NAMING OUR DESTINY

[handwritten signature]

NAMING OUR DESTINY
New and
Selected Poems

JUNE
JORDAN

Published in the United States by Thunder's Mouth
Press, 54 Greene Street, Suite 4S New York, N.Y.
10013

First printing 1989.

Library of Congress Cataloging-in-Publication Data:

Jordan, June, 1936–
    Naming our destiny ; new and selected poems / by June Jordan.
    p.   cm.
    ISBN 0-938410-83-0 ; $24.95. — ISBN 0-938410-84-9 (pbk.) ; $12.95
    I. Title.
    PS3560.073N3   1989   89-5070
    811'.54—dc20   CIP

Poems from *Things That I Do In the Dark* and
Passion © 1980, 1981 by June Jordan. Published in the
United Kingdom in *Lyrical Campaigns* (Virago Press,
1989). Reprinted by permission of Virago Press.

Poems from *Living Room* © 1985 by June Jordan.
First published in *Living Room* (Thunder's Mouth
Press, 1985).

The poet wishes to thank David Sheehan, and the
English Department of SUNY at Stony Brook, and
the MacDowell Colony for their indispensable, and
warm, support.

Grateful acknowledgment is made to the New York
State Council on the Arts and the National
Endowment for the Arts for financial assistance in the
publication of this work.

Designed by Marcia Salo

Printed in the United States of America

Distributed by Consortium Book Sales and
Distribution, Inc.
213 East 4th Street, St. Paul, Minn. 55101

For Tanzua
and
with my love and gratitude to
Mark Ainley, Sara Miles, and Adrienne Rich

These poems
they are things that I do
in the dark
reaching for you
whoever you are
and are you ready?

These words
they are stones in the water
running away

These skeletal lines
They are desperate arms for my longing and love.

I am a stranger
learning to worship the strangers
around me

whoever you are
whoever I may become.

Contents

PART TWO: from *Passion (1977—1980)*

PART THREE: from *Living Room (1980–1984)*

PART FOUR: *North Star (New Poems, 1985–1989)*

PART ONE

FROM
*Things that I Do
in the Dark*

Who Look at Me
Dedicated to my son, Christopher

Who would paint a people
black or white?

*

For my own I have held
where nothing showed me how
where finally I left alone
to trace another destination

*

A white stare splits the air
by blindness on the subway
in department stores
The Elevator
                (that unswerving ride
where man ignores the brother
by his side)

A white stare splits obliterates
the nerve-wrung wrist from work
the breaking ankle or
the turning glory
of a spine

*

Is that how we look to you
a partial nothing clearly real?

Who see a solid clarity
of feature
size and shape of some
one head
an unmistaken nose

the fact of afternoon
as darkening
his candle eyes

Older men with swollen neck
(when they finally sit down
who will stand up
for them?)

3

I cannot remember nor imagine pretty
people treat me
like a doublejointed stick
                    WHO LOOK AT ME
                    WHO SEE
the tempering sweetness
of a little girl who wears
her first pair of earrings
and a red dress

the grace of a boy removing
a white mask he makes beautiful

Iron grille across the glass
and frames of motion closed or
charred or closed

The axe lies on the ground
She listening to his coming sound

Him
just touching his feet
powerful and wary

anonymous and normal
parents and their offspring
posed in formal
                    *
I am
impossible to explain
remote from old and new interpretations
and yet
not exactly
                    *
look at the stranger as

he lies more gray than black
on that colorquilt
that
(everyone will say)
seems bright beside him

look
black sailors on the light
green sea the sky keeps blue

4

the wind blows high
and hard at night
for anyhow anywhere new
*
Who see starvation at the table
lines of men no work to do
my mother ironing a shirt?

Who see a frozen skin the midnight
of the winter and the hallway cold
to kill you like the dirt?

where kids buy soda pop
in shoeshine parlors
barber shops so they can hear
some laughing

Who look at me?

Who see the children
on their street the torn down door the wall
complete an early losing
                        games of ball
the search to find
a fatherhood a mothering of mind
a multimillion multicolored mirror
of an honest humankind?
*
look close
and see me black man mouth
for breathing (North and South)
A MAN

I am black alive and looking back at you.
*
see me brown girl throat
that throbs from servitude

see me hearing fragile
leap
and lead a black boy
reckless to succeed
to wrap my pride
around tomorrow and to go

there
without fearing

see me darkly covered ribs
around my heart across my skull
thin skin protects the part
that dulls from longing
*
Who see the block we face
the thousand miles of solid alabaster space
inscribed keep off keep out don't touch
and Wait Some More for Half as Much?
*
To begin is no more agony
than opening your hand
*
sometimes you have to dance
like spelling
the word joyless
*
Describe me broken mast
adrift but strong
regardless what may
come along
*
What do you suppose he hears
every evening?
*
I am stranded in a hungerland
of great prosperity
*
shelter happens seldomly and
like an accident
it stops
*
No doubt
the jail is white where I was born
but black will bail me out
*
We have lived as careful
as a church and prayer
in public
*

we reveal
a complicated past
of tinderbox and ruin
where we carried water
for the crops

we come from otherwhere

victim to a rabid cruel cargo crime

*to separate and rip apart
the trusting members of one heart*

my family

I looked for you
I looked for you
                 *
(slavery:) the insolence
                 *
came to frontiers
of paralyze highways
freedom strictly underground

came here to hatred hope labor love
and lynchlength rope

came a family to a family
                 *
I found my father
silently despite the grieving
fury of his life

Afternoons he wore his hat
and held a walking stick

I found my mother
her geography
becomes our home
                 *
so little safety
almost nowhere like the place
that childhood plans
in a pounding happy space
between deliberate brown and clapping
hands

that preached a reaping to the wildly
    sleeping earth
brown hands that worked for rain a fire inside
    and food to eat
from birth brown hands
    to hold
                    *
New energies of darkness we
disturbed a continent
like seeds

and life grows slowly
so we grew

We became a burly womb
an evening harvest kept by prayers
a hallelujah little room

We grew despite the crazy killing scorn
that broke the brightness to be born

In part we grew
by looking back at you

that white terrain
impossible for black America to thrive
that hostile soil to mazelike toil
backbreaking people into pain

we grew by work by waiting
to be seen
black face black body and black mind
beyond obliterating
homicide of daily insult daily death
the pistol slur the throbbing redneck war
with breath

In part we grew
with heroes who could halt a slaveship
lead the crew
like Cinque (son
of a Mendi African Chief) he
led in 1839
the Amistad Revolt

from slavehood forced
a victory he
killed the captain killed the cook
took charge
a mutiny for manhood
people
called him killer but
some
the Abolitionists
looked back at robbery
of person
murdering of spirit
slavery requires
and one
John Quincy Adams (seventy-three)
defended Cinque who
by highest court decree
in 1841 stood free
and freely he returned
to Africa
victorious

In part we grew
grandmother husband son
together when the laborblinding day was done

In part we grew
as we were meant to grow
ourselves
with kings and queens no white man knew

we grew by sitting on a stolen chair
by windows and a dream
by setting up a separate sail
to carry life
to start the song

to stop the scream
*
These times begin the ending of all lies
the fantasies of seasons start and stop
the circle leads to no surprise
for death does not bewilder

only life can kill can mystify can start
and stop like flowers ripening a funeral
like (people) holding hands across the knife
that cuts the casket to an extraordinary size
                    *
Tell the whiplash helmets GO!
and take away
that cream and orange Chevrolet
stripped to inside steel and parked
forever on one wheel

Set the wild dogs chewing up
that pitiful capitulation
plastic flower plastic draperies
to dust the dirt

Break the clothesline
Topple down the clotheslinepole

O My Lives Among The Wounded Buildings
should be dressed in trees and grass
                    *
we will no longer wait for want for watch
for what we will
                    *
we make a music marries room to room.
                    *
listen to that new girl
tears her party dress to sweep
the sidewalk as the elderly slow
preacher nears the mailbox in a black suit
emptyhanded
                    *
Although the world
forgets me
I will say yes
AND NO
                    *
NO
to a carnival run by freaks
who take a life
and tie it terrible
behind my back

10

No One Exists As Number Two
If you deny it you should try
being someone number two
                    *
I want to hear something other than a single
ringing on the concrete
                    *
I grieve the sorrow roar the sorrow sob
of many more left hand or right
black children and white
men the mountaintop the mob
I grieve the sorrow roar the sorrow sob
the fractured staring at the night

Sometimes America the shamescape
knock-rock territory losing shape
the Southern earth like blood
rolls valleys cold gigantic
weeping willow flood
that lunatic that lovely land
that graveyard growing
trees remark where men
another black man
died he died again
he died
                    *
I trust you will remember how we tried to love
above the pocket deadly need to please
and how so many of us died there
on our knees
                    *
Who see the roof and corners of my pride
to be (as you are) free?

WHO LOOK AT ME?

For My Jamaican Sister a Little Bit
Lost on the Island of Manhattan

small
and glowing in this cold place
of brick
   cement
   dry sand
   and
   broken glass
where there are waters
of the earth
flowing like love alive
you will make them warm
waters
hot (even)
like the delicate sweat
of tiger lilies
blowing about
barely in flame
          at sunrise

Juice of a Lemon on the Trail of
Little Yellow

Little Yellow looked at the banana tree and
he looked at the moon and he heard a banana tree baboon
beneath the moon and he sat on the grass
and fell asleep there

Little Yellow nine years old underneath the moon beside
a big banana tree smiled a mango smile as he
listened to a lullabye palm and a naked woman broke
coconuts for him and fed him meat from her mango
mammaries
Little Yellow curled himself in a large banana leaf
and he deeply sailed asleep toward the mango moon

Little Yellow traveled to a place where coolies worked
to build a bathtub for the rough and tribal Caribbean

There on that lush cerulean plateau and trapped he
was kept by his boss brother who positively took
out his teeth and left the mango mouth of Little Yellow
empty

One Minus One Minus One
*(This is a first map of territory I will have to explore as
poems, again and again)*

My mother murdering me
to have a life of her own

What would I say
(if I could speak about it?)

My father raising me
to be a life that he
owns

What can I say
(in this loneliness)

On The Spirit of Mildred Jordan

After sickness and a begging
from her bed
my mother dressed herself
grey lace-up oxfords
stockings baggy on her shrunken legs
an orange topper
rhinestone buttons
and a powder blue straw
hat with plastic
flowers

Then
she took the street
in short steps toward the corner

chewing gum
no less

she let the family laugh
again

she wasn't foxy
she was strong

Ah, Momma

Ah, Momma,

Did the house ever know the night-time of your spirit: the flash and
flame of you who once, when we crouched in what you called "the little
room," where your dresses hung in their pallid colorings—an unin-
teresting row of uniforms—and where there were dusty, sweet-
smelling boxes of costume jewelry that nevertheless shone like rubies,
gold, and diamonds, once, in that place where the secondhand mirror
blurred the person, dull, that place without windows, with doors
instead of walls, so that your small-space most resembled a large and
rather hazardous closet, once, in there you told me, whispering, that
once, you had wanted to be an artist: someone, you explained, who
could just boldly go and sit near the top of a hill and watch the setting of
the sun
Ah, Momma!
You said this had been your wish when you were quite as young as I was
then: a twelve- or thirteen-year-old girl who heard your confidence
with terrified amazement: what had happened to you and your wish?
Would it happen to me too?

Ah, Momma:
    "The little room" of your secrets, your costumery, perfumes and
photographs of an old boyfriend you did not marry (for reasons not
truly clear to me as I saw you make sure, time after time, that his
pictures were being kept as clean and as safely as possible)—"the little

room" adjoined the kitchen, the kitchen where no mystery survived, except for the mystery of you: woman who covered her thick and long, black hair with a starched, white nurse's cap when she went "on duty" away from our home into the hospital I came to hate, jealously, woman who rolled up her wild and heavy, beautiful hair before she went to bed, woman who tied a headrag around the waving, kinky, well-washed braids, or lengthy, fat curls of her hair while she moved, without particular grace or light, between the table and the stove, between the sink and the table, around and around and around in the spacious, ugly kitchen where she, where you, never dreamed about what you were doing or what you might do instead, and where you taught me to set down plates and silverware, and even fresh-cut flowers from the garden, without appetite, without excitement, without expectation.

It was not there, in that obvious, open, square cookery where you spent most of the hours of the days, it was not there, in the kitchen where nothing ever tasted sweet or sharp enough to sate the yearnings I began to suspect inside your eyes, and also inside the eyes of my father, it was not there that I began to hunger for the sun as my own, legitimate preoccupation; it was not there, in the kitchen, that I began, really, to love you
Ah, Momma,
It was where I found you, hidden away, in your "little room," where your life and the power, the rhythms of your sacrifice, the ritual of your bowed head, and your laughter always partly concealed, where all of you, womanly, reverberated big as the whole house, it was there that I came, humbly, into an angry, an absolute determination that I would, one day, prove myself to be, in fact, your daughter
Ah, Momma, I am still trying

From The Talking Back of Miss Valentine Jones: Poem # one

well I wanted to braid my hair
bathe and bedeck my
self so fine
so fully aforethought for
your pleasure
see:
I wanted to travel and read

and runaround fantastic
into war and peace:
I wanted to
surf
dive
fly
climb
conquer
and be conquered
THEN
I wanted to pickup the phone
and find you asking me
if I might possibly be alone
some night
(so I could answer cool
as the jewels I would wear
on bareskin for your
digmedaddy delectation:)
"WHEN
you comin ova?"
But
I had to remember to write down
margarine on the list
and shoepolish and a can of
sliced pineapples in casea company
and a quarta skim milk cause Teresa's
gaining weight and don' nobody groove on
that much
girl
and next I hadta sort for darks and lights before
the laundry hit the water which I had
to kinda keep a eye on be-
cause if the big hose jumps the sink again that
Mrs. Thompson gointa come upstairs
and brain me with a mop don' smell too
nice even though she hang
it headfirst out the winda
and I had to check
on William like to
burn hisself to death with fever
boy so thin be
callin all day "Momma! Sing to me?"

"Ma! Am I gone die?" and me not
wake enough to sit beside him longer than
to wipeaway the sweat or change the sheets/
his shirt and feed him orange
juice before I fall out sleep and
Sweet My Jesus ain but one can
left
and we not thru the afternoon
and now
you (temporarily) shownup with a thing
you say's a poem and you
call it
"Will The Real Miss Black America Standup?"

       guilty po' mouth
       about duty beauties of my
       headrag
       boozedup doozies about
       never mind
       cause love is blind

well
I can't use it

and the very next bodacious Blackman
call me queen
because my life ain shit
because (in any case) he ain been here to share it
with me
(dish for dish and do for do and
dream for dream)
I'm gone scream him out my house
be-
cause what I wanted was
to braid my hair/bathe and bedeck my
self so fully be-
cause what I wanted was
your love
not pity
be-
cause what I wanted was
your love
your love

The Wedding

Tyrone married her this afternoon
not smiling as he took the aisle
and her slightly rough hand.
Dizzella listened to the minister
staring at his wrist and twice
forgetting her name:
Do you promise to obey?
Will you honor humility and love
as poor as you are?
Tyrone stood small but next
to her person
trembling. Tyrone stood
straight and bony
black alone with one key
in his pocket.
By marrying today
they made themselves a man
and woman
answered friends or unknown
curious about the Cadillacs
displayed in front of Beaulah Baptist.
Beaulah Baptist
life in general
indifferent
barely known
nor caring to consider
the earlywed Tyrone
and his Dizella
brave enough
but only two.

The Reception

Doretha wore the short blue lace last night
and William watched her drinking so she fight
with him in flying collar slim-jim orange
tie and alligator belt below the navel pants uptight

"I flirt. You hear me? Yes I flirt.
Been on my pretty knees all week
to clean the rich white downtown dirt
the greedy garbage money reek.

I flirt. Damned right. You look at me."
But William watched her carefully
his mustache shaky she could see
him jealous, "which is how he always be

at parties." Clementine and Wilhelmina
looked at trouble in the light blue lace
and held to Geroge while Roosevelt Senior
circled by the yella high and bitterly light blue face

he liked because she worked
the crowded room like clay like molding men
from dust to muscle jerked
and arms and shoulders moving when

she moved. The Lord Almighty Seagrams bless
Doretha in her short blue dress
and Roosevelt waiting for his chance:
a true gut-funky blues to make her really dance.

Roman Poem Number Eight

He ordered a beer
She ordered a beer
I asked for apricot
yoghurt
        "You know this game?
Nothing personal. For instance
June is all bird
but you," he spoke
to my rival, "You
are half-horse-half-
butterfly."
            "Why
do you say I'm a bird?"

"Always up in the head
thinking
far from the earth."

I had been counting
the hairs on his wrist
but today
since he has been really
riding his horse
I venture to startle
the hairs of his arm
and listen to the thick
crackling
of his
persistent sex.

Roman Poem Number Thirteen
For Eddie

Only our hearts will argue hard
against the small lights letting in the news
and who can choose between the worst possibility
and the last
between the winners of the wars against the breathing
and the last
war everyone will lose
and who can choose between the dry gas
domination of the future
and the past
between the consequences of the killers
and the past
of all the killing? There
is no choice in these.
Your voice
breaks very close to me my love.

Roman Poem Number Fourteen

believe it love
believe
      my lover
lying down he
lifts me up and high
and I am
high on him

believe it love
believe

the carnage scores around
the corner

o believe it love
believe

the bleeding fills the carnage cup
my lover lifts me
I am up
      and love is lying down

believe
believe it

crazies wear a clean shirt to the fire
o my lover
lift me higher higher

crazies take a scream and
make a speech they talk and
wash their mouths in dirt
no love will hurt
me lover lift me lying down

believe
believe it
carnage crazies
snap smash more more
(what you waiting for?)
you own the rope knife rifles the whole list
the searing bomb starch brighteners
the nuclear family whiteners

look the bridge be fallen down
look the ashes from the bones turn brown
look the mushroom hides the town
look the general wears his drip dry red
drip gown

o my lover nakedly
believe my love

believe
believe it

For My Brother

Teach me to sing
Blackman Blacklove
sing when the cops break your head
full of song
sing when the bullets explode in the back
you bend over me
Blacklove Blackman
sing when you empty the world
to fill up the needles that kill
needles killing you
killing
you
teach me to sing
Blackman Blacklove
teach me to sing.

It's About You:
On the Beach

You have
two hands absolutely lean and clean
to let go the gold
the silver flat or plain rock

sand
but hold the purple pieces
atom articles
that glorify a color
yours is orange
oranges are like you love
a promising
a calm skin and a juice
inside
a juice
a running from the desert
Lord
see how you run
YOUR BODY IS A LONG BLACK WING
YOUR BODY IS A LONG BLACK WING

Of Nightsong and Flight

There are things lovely and dangerous still

the rain
when the heat of an evening
sweetens the darkness with mist

and the eyes cannot see what the memory will
of new pain

when the headlights deceive
like the windows wild birds believe to be air
and bash bodies and wings
on the glass

when the headlights show space
but the house and the room and the bed and your face
are still there
while I am mistaken
and try to drive by

the actual kiss
of the world everywhere

About Long Distances on Saturday

he calls me from his house and
the timing seems bad
and I offer to call him back
later
but he says "no"
I'm about to split for the weekend
so
call me yeah
early next week or
sometime
and the answer is
that the question
is

(isn't it)

where are you going
baby

without me?

Calling on All Silent Minorities

HEY

C'MON
COME OUT

WHEREVER YOU ARE

WE NEED TO HAVE THIS MEETING
AT THIS TREE

AIN' EVEN BEEN
PLANTED
YET

No Poem Because Time Is Not a Name

But beyond the
anxiety
the
querulous and reckless intersecting
conflict
and the trivial misleading banal
and separating fences every scrim
disguise each mask and feint
red herrings broadside poor
maneuvers of the
begging
hopeful
heart that wants and waits the
head that works against the minute
minute
There are pictures/memories of
temperature or cast or tone
or hue and vision
pictures of a dream
and dreams of memories and
dreams of gardens dreams of film
and pictures
of the daring
simple
fabulous
bold
difficult
and distant
inextricable
main
nigger
that I love
and
this is not
a poem

On a New Year's Eve

Infinity doesn't interest me

not altogether
anymore

I crawl and kneel and grub about
I beg and listen for

what can go away

                    (as easily as love)

or perish
like the children
running
hard on oneway streets/infinity
doesn't interest me

not anymore

not even
repetition your/my/eye-
lid or the colorings of sunrise
or all the sky excitement
added up

is not enough

to satisfy this lusting adulation that I feel
for
your brown arm before it
moves

MOVES
CHANGES UP

the temporary sacred
tales ago
first bikeride round the house
when you first saw a squat
opossum
carry babies on her back

opossum up
in the persimmon tree
you reeling toward
that natural
first
absurdity
with so much wonder still
it shakes your voice

                    the temporary is the sacred
                    takes me out

and even the stars and even the snow and even
the rain
do not amount to much
unless these things submit to some disturbance
some derangement such
as when I yield myself/belonging
to your unmistaken
body

and let the powerful lock up the canyon/mountain
peaks the
hidden rivers/waterfalls the
deepdown minerals/the coalfields/goldfields/
diamond mines close by the whoring ore
hot
at the center of the earth

spinning fast as numbers
I cannot imagine

let the world blot
obliterate remove so-
called
magnificence
so-called
almighty/fathomless and everlasting
treasures/
wealth
(whatever that may be)
it is this time
that matters

it is this history
I care about

the one we make together
awkward
inconsistent
as a lame cat on the loose
or quick as kids freed by the bell
or else as strictly
once
as only life must mean
a once upon a time

I have rejected propaganda teaching me
about the beautiful
the truly rare

(supposedly
the soft push of the ocean at the hushpoint of the shore
supposedly
the soft push of the ocean at the hushpoint of the shore
is beautiful
for instance)
but
the truly rare can stay out there

I have rejected that
abstraction that enormity
unless I see a dog walk on the beach/
a bird seize sandflies
or yourself
approach me
laughing out a sound to spoil
the pretty picture
make an uncontrolled
heartbeating memory
instead

I read the papers preaching on
that oil and oxygen
that redwoods and the evergreens
that trees the waters and the atmosphere
compile a final listing of the world in
short supply

but all live and all the lives
persist perpetual
in jeopardy
persist
as scarce as every one of us
as difficult to find
or keep
as irreplaceable
as frail
as every one of us

and
as I watch your arm/your
brown arm
just
before it moves

I know

all things are dear
that disappear

*all things are dear
that disappear*

For Ethelbert

if I cda known youd be real
back in them supreme court
gonna rule all evil out
days
I wda rushd to judgment
(lordy lord)
rushd thru
to the fiery seat itselve
and stayd there
cool as any momma madeup
her holy/everlastin min'
(chile *honey!*)
and sed

"sentence me, please,
to a long life long
enough
so's I gets to meet
what's comin afta (this mess)"
meanin'
you

For Dave: 1976

There wasn't any hot water for the teapot
so you came by to fix the furnace
and you found me
"very pretty" (you said)
underneath my worries

Leaving the wind behind the door you came
and when you left to sleep elsewhere
you left me ready to keep on
dancing by myself

I was accustomed to the Army cap that spills your
hair below those clean-as-a-whistle ears nobody
knows how to blow so you can hear them honest-to-
God
But I was a stranger to your hair let free your arms
around me
reading my lips then licking them gentle as a bear
sure that he hugs a honey tree not going anywhere
(which is true: for you
                              washing up with Ajax
leaving the rifle outside the way the Japanese
leave shoes
catching eels to smoke them good enough to eat
rebuilding a friend's house "after work")

Now you were lifting me as easily as we could laugh
between ourselves
you wanting to know what I was thinking about

me wanting to tell but unwilling to shout
at you (so you could hear me)

You arrive (red shirt
            new shoes
            the shower shining everywhere about you)
And I accept again
that there are simple ways of being joined
to someone
absolutely different from myself
And I admire the forthright
crocus first to mitigate the winter
with its thrust voluptuous/
on time

I mean to say
that it's not talk that brings us close together
and
thank god!

Meta-Rhetoric

Homophobia
racism
self-definition
revolutionary struggle

the subject tonight for
public discussion is
our love

we sit apart
apparently at opposite ends of a line
and I feel the distance
between my eyes
between my legs
a dry
dust topography of our separation

In the meantime people
dispute the probabilities
of union

They reminisce about the chasmic histories
no ideology yet dares to surmount

I disagree with you
You disagree with me
The problem seems to be a matter of scale

Can you give me the statistical dimensions
of your mouth on my mouth
your breasts resting on my own?

I believe the agenda involves
several inches (at least)
of coincidence and endless recovery

My hope is that our lives will declare
this meeting
open

On the Loss of Energy
(and other things)

no more the chicken and the egg come

one of them
before the other
both
be fadin (steady)
from the supersafeway/a & p/giant
circus

      uh-huh
      the pilgrim cornucopia
      it ain' a pot to pee in
      much
      (these days)

gas is gone
and alka seltza runnin gas
a close race

outasight/you
name it
        toilet paper
        halfway honest politicians
there's shortage
folks/*please*
step right up)
a crisis
(*come in closer*)
A International Disaster
Definitely Takin Place
(give the little lady down in front some room)
and (*how about the brother in the back row/can
you hear me brother?*)
                        WELL
                        I SAID THE HOT AIR'S RUNNIN
                        OUTASTEAM
                        I SAID
                        THE MEAT'S NOT GOOD
                        FOR KIDS TO EAT
                        TOO FULLAFAT
                        AND STUFF LIKE THAT
                        AND
                        IF YOU EAT MEAT
                        HOW YOU PLAN TO PAY THE
                            RENT?
                        I SAID
                        THE OILWELLS DRIBBLIN
                        LOWER THAN A SNAKE
                        AND SOON WON'T BE NO HEAT
                        AND SO YOU MIGHT AS WELL
                            EAT MEAT
                        EXCEPT THERE AINT NO
                        MEAT TO EAT
                        I SAID

                        BROTHER CAN YOU SPARE A
                            DIME?

these things/they gettin more and more worse in
the time it takes to tell
you

how the country's bound to hell
you
first
if you be middlin poor or poor or Black or Black-and-poor
this profit-makin mess the worst
mess we been force to handle
since the civil war
close down the crackers
reconstructed
how the north won
into victory the crackers like to celebrate/a
reconstruction of the facts
on poor and Blackbacks
but
I am digressin/*folks*
please settle down and listen good
I say you know
you know
the affluent society
starvin high
on the hog as pigs can get
I say you know
we all been pigs
but mostly we been little pigs/I say
the big pigs
got the whole big pigpen
underneath some tasty big-pig pigs' feet
dynamite can move
where is the dynamite?
How come we tryin to cooperate
with this "emergency"/this faker/phony
ripoff
got you plannin
not to die and not to have a baby
on the weekends
not to do too much/
much less to start to die or start to have
a baby
on a Sunday
or on early Monday
got you/stiff and slow and hungry
on them lines the richboys laugh about/

Will somebody
real and prominent and smart
please stand
up here
and tell about inequities and big and little pigs
and other animals and birds/and fish
don't know a thing about no hog behavior/*where's*
the dynamite?
I say you know/I say
you know.
And so do I.

What Would I Do White?

What would I do white?
What would I do clearly full
of not exactly beans nor
pearls my nose a manicure
my eyes a picture of your wall?

I would disturb the streets by
passing by so pretty kids
on stolen petty cash would look
at me like foreign
writing in the sky
I would forget my furs on any chair.
I would ignore the doormen at the knob
the social sanskrit of my life
unwilling to disclose my cosmetology,
I would forget.

Over my wine I would acquire
I would inspire big returns to equity
the equity of capital I am
accustomed to accept

like wintertime.

I would do nothing.
That would be enough.

In Memoriam:
Martin Luther King, Jr.

I
honey people murder mercy U.S.A.
the milkland turn to monsters teach
to kill to violate pull down destroy
the weakly freedom growing fruit
from being born

America

tomorrow yesterday rip rape
exacerbate despoil disfigure
crazy running threat the
deadly thrall
appall belief dispel
the wildlife burn the breast
the onward tongue
the outward hand
deform the normal rainy
riot sunshine shelter wreck
of darkness derogate
delimit blank
explode deprive
assassinate and batten up
like bullets fatten up
the raving greed
reactivate a springtime
terrorizing

death by men by more
than you or I can

STOP

II
They sleep who know a regulated place
or pulse or tide or changing sky
according to some universal
stage direction obvious
like shorewashed shells

we share an afternoon of mourning
in between no next predictable
except for wild reversal hearse rehearsal
bleach the blacklong lunging
ritual of fright insanity and more
deplorable abortion
more and
more

For Michael Angelo Thompson
(October 25, 1959–March 23, 1973)

So Brooklyn has become a holy place

the streets have turned to meadowland
where
wild
free
ponies
eat among the wild
free
flowers
growing there

Please do not forget.

A tiger does not fall or stumble
broken by an accident
A tiger does not lose his stride or
clumsy
slip and slide to tragedy
that buzzards feast upon.

Do not forget.

The Black prince Michael Black boy
our young brother
has not "died"
he
has not "passed away"

the Black prince Michael Black boy

our young brother

>   He was killed.
>   He did not die.

It was the city took him off
(that city bus)
and smashed him suddenly
to death
deliberate.

It was the city took him off
the hospital
that turned him down the hospital
that turned away from so much beauty
bleeding
bleeding
in Black struggle
>   just to live.
It was the city took him off
the casket names and faces
of the hatred spirit
stripped the force the
laughter and the agile power
of the child

>   He did not die.
>   A tiger does not fall.
>   Do not forget.

The streets have turned to meadowland
where
wild
free
ponies
eat among the wild
free
flowers
growing there

and Brooklyn
has become a holy place.

On Moral Leadership
as a Political Dilemma
(Watergate, 1973)

I don't know why but
I cannot tell a lie

I chopped down the cherry tree
I did
I did that
yessirree
I chopped down the cherry tree

and to tell you the truth
see
that was only in the morning

which left a whole day and part
of an evening (until suppertime)
to continue doing what I like to do
about cherry trees

which is

to chop them down

then pick the cherries
and roll them into a cherry-pie circle
and then
stomp the cherries
stomp them
jumping up and down

hard and heavy
jumping up to stomp them
so the flesh leaks and the juice
runs loose
and then I get to pick at the pits
or else I pick up the cherry pits
(depending on my mood)
and then
I fill my mouth completely full
of cherry pits
and run over to the river

the Potomac
where I spit
the cherry pits
47 to 65 cherry pits spit
into the Potomac
at one spit

and to tell you the truth some more
if I ever see a cherry tree
standing around no matter where
and here let me please be perfectly clear
no matter where
I see a cherry tree
standing around
even if it belongs to a middle-American of
moderate means with a two-car family
that is falling apart in a respectable
civilized
falling apart
mind-your-manners manner

even then
or even if you happen to be
corporate rich or
unspeakably poor or famous
or fashionably thin or comfortably fat
or even as peculiar as misguided as
a Democrat

or even a Democrat

even then
see
if you have a cherry tree
and I see it
I will chop that cherry tree down
stomp the cherries
fill my mouth completely with the pits to
spit them into the Potomac
and I don't know why
it is
that I cannot tell a lie

but that's the truth.

40

Uhuru *in the O.R.*

The only successful heart transplant, of the first five attempts, meant that a black heart kept alive a white man—a white man who upheld apartheid.

I like love anonymous
more than murder incorporated or
shall we say South Africa
I like the Valentine the heart the power
incorruptible but failing body
flowers of the world

From my death the white man
takes new breath he stands as
formerly he stood and he commands me
for his good he overlooks
my land my people
in transition transplantations
hearts   and power
beating beating beating beating
hearts in transplantation
power in transition

If You Saw a Negro Lady

If you saw a Negro lady
sitting on a Tuesday
near the whirl-sludge doors of
Horn & Hardart on the main drag
of downtown Brooklyn

solitary and conspicuous as plain
and neat as walls impossible to
fresco and you watched her self-
conscious features shape about
a Horn & Hardart teaspoon
with a pucker from a cartoon

she would not understand
with spine as straight and solid
as her years of bending over floors
allowed

skin cleared of interest by a ruthless
soap   nails square and yellowclean
from metal files

sitting in a forty-year-old-flush
of solitude and prickling
from the new white cotton blouse
concealing nothing she had ever noticed
even when she bathed and never
hummed a bathtub tune nor knew one

If you saw her square
above the dirty
mopped-on antiseptic floors
before the rag-wiped table tops

little finger   broad and stiff
in heavy emulation of a cockney
mannerism
would you turn her treat
into surprise
observing

happy birthday

Roman Poem Number Five
For Millen and for Julius
and for Peter and for Eddie

1
This is a trip that strangers make
a journey ending on the beach where things
come together like four fingers on his
rather predictable

spine exposed by stars and
when he said this
has never happened before he
meant something
specific to himself because he could not
meet me anywhere inside but
you know
we were both out of the water
both out of it
and really what we wanted was
to screw ourselves into
the place

Pompeii
the Sarno River to the south
the mountain of Vesuvius to the north
the river did not burn
none of the records indicate
a burning river

      of all that went before the earth
      remembers nothing

             everywhere you see
      the fertility of its contempt
      the sweet alyssum blooming
      in the tomb

      an inward town
well suited to the lives
unraveled and undone
despite the secretly coloring
interior of their suddenly blasted
walls

Vesuvius created and destroyed
           WHOLE TOP OF THE
              MOUNTAIN
           BLOWN OFF
           you can hum some words
           catchy like the title of a song
           (a little song)

WHOLE TOP OF THE
MOUNTAIN
BLOWN OFF

**(play it again
sam)**

Pompeii
the mountain truly coming to the men
who used to walk these streets these
sewer drains (the difference is
not very clear)

> juniper and cypress trees
> inspire the dark the only definite the trying
> forms on the horizon sky and sea and the Bay
> of Naples
> single trees
> against abstraction
> trees

the mainstreet moves directly
to the mouth the mountaintop
a vicious puckering

> This is a place where all the lives
> are planted in the ground
> the green things grow
> the other ones
> volcanic victims of an overflow
> a fireflushing tremble
> soul unseasonal
> in rush and rapture
> well they do not grow
> they seed the rest of us
> who prowl
> with plundersucking polysyllables
> to rape the corpse
> to fuck the fallen down and died
> long time ago
> again

his hand removes some of the sand on my neck
with difficulty

> did the river did the river burn

Pliny the Younger who delivered the volcano
who arrested the eruption into words
excited arrogant terrific
an exclusive
elegant account of mass destruction
79 A.D. that Johnny-on-the-spot say nothing
much about the river and
but eighteen is not too old to worry
for the rivers of the world
                              around the apple flesh and fit

loves holds easily
the hard skin soft enough

                    picture him sweet but cold
                    above the eyebrows
                    just a teenage witness with his pencil
                    writing down disaster

some say
put that apple into uniform
the tree itself wears buttons
in the spring
            VISITING DISASTER IS A WEIRD IDEA
            WHETHER YOU THINK ABOUT IT OR
            NOT

for example limestone the facade the statues the limestone statues of
the everyone of them dead and dead and dead and no more face among
the buried under twenty-seven feet of limestone other various in
general all kinds of dust covering the dead the finally comfortable
statues of the dusty smell today the nectar fragrance the sun knocks
down my meter taking notes the wheel ruts gutter drains the overhang-
ing upperstories the timber superstructure the dead the very dead the
very very dead dead farmland pasture dead potato chip dead rooms of
the dead the no longer turbulent blazing the no longer glorious
inglorious the finish of the limestone building limestone statues look at
the wild morninglories red and yellow laughter at the dying who dig
into the death of limestone hard to believe the guide leads people to the
public baths I Bagni di Publicci to talk about slaves and masters and
how many sat at table he explains the plumbing where men bathed and
where the women (bathed) hot water cold where the wall has a hole in it
or where there is no hole in the wall and the tourists listening and

nobody asks him a question how about the living and the dead how
about that

Pompeii
and we are people who notice the mosaic decorations
of a coffin

we claim to be ordinary men and women or
extraordinary
elbows touching
cameras ready
sensible shoes
architects archaeologists classical
scholars one poet
Black and White and Jewish and Gentile and partly young
and married and once or twice married but
why do we follow
all
inquisitive
confessional or
necrophilomaniac or anyhow
alone
I am not here for you and I will stay there
we are disturbing the peace of the graveyard and
that is the believable limit of our impact
our intent
no
tonight he will hold me hard on the rocks of the ground
if the weather is warm and if
it doesn't rain

2
KEEP MOVING KEEP MOVING

the past is practically
behind us

half skull and teeth
knocked down running an
extreme tilt jerk tilted skull
stiff on its pole plaster cartilage
the legs apart like elbows
then the arms themselves the mouth

46

of the dead man tense defending still
the visitors peruse these plaster
memories of people
forms created in the cinders
living visitors admire the poise
of agony the poise of agony is
absolute
and who would call it sculpture
raise your own hand to the fire

                              IN THE VILLA DEI
                                  MISTERI
                              THERE ARE BLACK
                                  WALLS

another plaster person
crouched into his suffocation

yes well in the 14th century B.C.
they had this remarkable
bedroom where
they would keep one bed
or (some authorities say)
two beds
maybe it was the 15th

                         Pompeii
                         the unfamiliar plain
                         the unfamiliar guilt
                         annihilated men and women who
                         most likely
                         never heard of archaeology of
                         dusty lust

all the possible homes were never built
(repeat)
"What's that?"

"That's a whorehouse, honey."

freckle hands chafing together
urbane
he tells the group that in
the declinium

women stayed apart with their loom
(in the declinium

occasional among the rocks the buttercups
obscure until the devil of the land)

        Perhaps Aristotle said the size
        of a city
        should take a man's shout to ears
        even on the edge
        but size never took anything
        much no matter what the porno
        makes believe but
        what will take in the
        scream of a what will
        take it in?

current calculations postulate the
human beings half the size of the market
place

        BEES
        LIZARDS

walls plus walls inhibit action on the lateral
or
with all them walls now how
you gone get next to me

        the falling of ashes
        the rolling lava

the way the things be happening
that garden story figleaf it belong
on top your head

        they had these industries these
        wool and fish sauce
        ways to spend the
        fooler

        even the moon is dark among us
        except for the lights by the mountainside
        except for the lights

20,000 people
subject
to Vesuvius in natural violence blew
up the handicrafted
fortress spirit of Pompeii
the liquid mangling
motley blood and lava
subject
20,000 people

KEEP MOVING KEEP MOVING

to them the theatre was "indispensable"
seats for 5,000 fabulous acoustics
what
was the performance of the people
in surprise
the rhythm chorus speaking
rescue
multitudes to acrobat survival
one last action on that last
entire stage
       today the cypress tree tips dally
       wild above the bleachers

when it happened what is happening to us
to hell with this
look at the vegetables blue
in the moonlight

       a pinetree colonnade
       the wall just under
       and the one man made

come to Pompeii
touch my tongue with yours
study the cold formulation of a fearful fix
grid patterns to the streets
the boundaries "unalterable"

the rights of property in stone
the trapezoidal plot the signals
of possession

laughter
(let's hear it loud)
the laughing of the lava
tell me
stern
rigid
corpulent
stories

the mountains surround the wastebasket bricks of our inquiry

in part
the waters barely stir with poison or with fish

I think I know
the people who
were here
where I am

3
my love completely and
one evening anywhere
I will arrive
the right way
given
up to you
and keep no peace
my body sings the force
of your disturbing legs

WHAT DID YOU SAY?
NO THANKS.
WHAT DID YOU SAY?

Vesuvius
when Daddy Adam did what he did
the blame the bliss beginning
of no thanks
this is a bad connection
are you serious?

the river did not burn

the group goes on
among the bones we travel

50

light into a new
starvation

        Pompeii was yesterday
here is Herculaneum
a second interesting testimony
to excuse me but how
will you try to give testimony
to a mountain?

        there it is baby there it is
        FURTHER EXCAVATION INTO
        HERCULANEUM
        ARRESTED TODAY BY RESSINI living
        inhabitants impoverished the non-
        descript Ressini town on top the
        ruins of

amazing Herculaneum
constructed on an earlier rehearsal flow
of lava maybe
courage or like that a seashore
a resort the remnant spread the
houses under houses
tall trees underlying grass the
pine and palm trees spring toward
Ressini grass retaining walls against the water
where there is no water and the sound of children
crying from which city is it Ressini is it
Herculaneum that
does not matter does it is it
the living or the visited the living or
the honored ERCOLANO

        SUCK
        SUCK HARD

"Here's where they sold spaghetti"
the leafy sound the feel
of the floor the tile
the painting of a wineglass
a wineglass on the wall unprecedented
turquoise colors would
the red walls make you warm
in winter

INFORMATION
WAS
NOT AVAILABLE
THE POOR
OF RESSINI
REFUSE
TO COOPERATE
WITH AUTHORITIES

you better watch out
next summer
and Ressini gone slide

        down inside them fancy
        stones
        and stay there
        using
        flashlight
        or whatever

NOBODY BUDGE
KEEP MOVING KEEP MOVING

        cabbages cauliflower broccoli
        the luminous leaves on the land

4
yesterday and yesterday
Paestum dates from four
hundred fifty years before the Christ
a fertile lowland calmly naked
and the sky excites the rubble flowers
in between
the mountains and the water
bleaching gentle
in the Middle Ages
mountainstreams came down
and made the meadow into marsh
marble travertine deposits when
the mountains left the land
the memory
deranged the water
turned the plants
to stone

52

this is the truth the people left this place alone

        we are somewhere wounded by the wind
        a mystery
        a stand deserted by the trees

drizzling rain
destroys the dandelion
and your lips enlarge the glittering
of silence

        Paestum dedicated temples dedicated
        to the terra cotta figurines of trust
        the women in becoming mother of the world
        the midwives hold her arms
        like wings

the river does not burn

        delivering the life

the temple does not stand
still

        PERMISSION GRANTED TO PRESENT
        STONE SEX THE ECSTASY OF
        PAESTUM

4 main rows of
six in front
the tapering the girth the groove
the massive lifted fit of things
the penis worshiping
fecundity
fecundity
the crepis
stylobate
the cella
columns in entasis
magic
diminution
Doric
flutes
entablature
the leaning

curvilinear
the curve
the profile
magic
elasticity
diameter
effacement

THE TEMPLE IS THE COLOR OF A LIFE

ON STONE THE SUN CONTINUES
BLISTERING THE SURFACE
TENDERLY

WHAT TIME IS IT?

as we approach each other
someone else is making
a movie
there are horses
one or two beautiful men
and
birds flying
away

Roman Poem Number Six

You walk downstairs
to see this man who moves so
quietly in a dark room
where there are balancing
scales on every table.
Signore D'Ettore can tell
you anything about
communications if you mean
the weight the price
of letters
packages
and special post cards.

Hunch-back
short
his grey hair always groomed
meticulous
with a comb and just a touch
of grease
            for three months
he has worn the same well
tailored suit
a grey suit quite unlike
his hair.
            I find it restful
just to watch him making
judgements all of us accept.
"But are you sad?", he asks
me looking up.

"The world is beautiful
but men are bad," he says in
slow Italian.
I smile with him but still the problem
is not solved.
The photographs of Rome
must reach my father but the big
official looking book seems blank
the finger-nail of Signore D'Ettore
seems blind and wandering
from line to line among the countries
of a long
small-printed list.
"Jamaica? Where is Jamaica?"
I am silent. My Italian
is not good enough to say, "Jamaica
is an island where you can find
calypso roses sunlight and an old man
my father
on his knees."

About Enrique's Drawing

She lies down a mess
on white paper under glass
a long and a short leg a twisted
arm one good and even
muscular
an okay head
but body in a bloat
impossible

       "NO! Not impossible," he says
        standing.
      "It is
         a body.
      It is
         a structure
         that   is not
                regular.
                    Do you see?
                        No?

    Listen:
        ONE
        ONE
        ONE TWO
        THREE FOUR
        ONE
        ONE
        ONETWOTHREE
        ONETWOTHREE
        ONE TWO
        ONETWOTHREE
        ONE TWO
        THREE FOUR
        ONE
        ONE. . . ."

Enrique's body
has become the structure
of a dance. He is real.
And she

the woman lying down a mess
she
has become
mysterious.

On Declining Values

In the shadows of the waiting room
are other shadows
beaten
elderly women or
oldfolk bums
depending on your point of view

but
all depending

formerly mothers formerly wives
formerly citizens of some acceptable
position
but
depending and
depending
now exposed unable and unwashed
a slow and feeble crawling through the city
varicose
veins bulging
while the arteries the intake systems
harden
wither
shrivel
close
depending and depending

II
She will leave Grand Central Station
and
depending
spend two hours in St. Patrick's

if the guards there
if police ignore the grovelling length
of time it takes
a hungry woman
just to pray

but here
she whispers
with an aging boyfriend
fugitive and darkblue suited out
for begging who
has promised her a piece
of candy or an orange or an apple
if
they meet tomorrow
if the cops don't chase them separated
wandering under thin
gray hair

III
meanwhile
cops come quick
knockbopping up the oakwood benches
BANG
BOP
"GET OUTAHERE," they shout around
the ladies women sisters dying old and all
the formerly wives and mothers
shuffle soft
away
with paper shopping bags beside them
almost empty
and a medium young man
comes up
to ask a question:
"Tell me, I mean, seriously,
how does it feel to be beautiful?"

And I look back at him
a little bit alarmed
a little bit amused
before I say:

"It all depends too much
on you."

Some People

Some people despise me be-
cause I have a Venus mound
and not a penis

Does that *sound*
right
to you?

Fragments from a Parable
Paul was Saul. Saul got on the road and the road
and somebody else changed him into somebody else
on the road.

The worst is not knowing if I do take somebody's
word on it means I don't know and you have to believe
if you just don't know. How do I dare to stand as
still as I am still standing? Arrows create me.
And I despise directions. I am no wish.
After all the lunging still
myself is no sanctuary
birds feed and fly inside me shattering
the sullen spell of my desiring and the
accidental conquest.
Eyeless wings will
twist and sting
the tree of my remaining
like the wind.
Always there is not knowing, not knowing everything
of myself and having to take whoever you are at your
word. About me.

I am she.

And this is my story of Her. The story is properly yours to tell. You have created Her, but carelessly. As large as a person, she nevertheless learns why she walks and the aim of her gaze and the force of her breath from you who coax her to solve independently the mystery of your making: Her self.

Your patterns deny parenthood; deny every connection suggesting a connection; a consequence. She cannot discover how she began nor how she may begin. She seeks the authority of birth. Her fails.

Launched or spinning politely she fails to become her as self unless you allow her a specialty she will accept as her reason for being. Perhaps you allow her a skill like mercy or torment. The particular means nothing. Your approval matters like life and death. She is who I am.

I am.

My name is me. I am what you call black. (Only I am still. Arrest me. Arrest me any one or thing. If you arrest me I am yours. I am yours ready for murder or am I yours ready to expose any closed vein. Which is not important. Am I matter to you? Does it? You will try when. But now I am never under arrest. Meanwhile that slit allows me concentration on the bricks black between the windows. I am one of those suffering frozen to the perpetual corrosion of me. Where is the stillness that means?)

Here am I holding a pen with two fingers of frenzy of stream of retreat of connection and neurons. Supposedly there is a synapse between things like this: A difference:

between
beyond
beneath

illusions

At least a space without pulse. Without illusion: Only I am still: Only I am remaining. I repeat: I am not still: I repeat: Arrest me! You would say mine is a monotone if I could keep my tongue in my fist and my fist in my mouth and my mouth in a glass and that glass in my eyes. But monotony resonates: That would prove how merely am i a complicated position. Or riveted respectably with foot to the ground ignoring the drum and the furnace, the seeds and the water then could I say I am still pretending to be still.

But that complicated position is not. I was simply conceived by something like love. I was simply conceived during the war. My mother was the most beautiful woman in the world. My father was a macrosperm of lust for that woman painfully asleep on the battlefield. This lust, this loving uncertainty seized three hundred soldiers who paused at her silence as she lay. They made their rabid inquiry and left her.

For almost a year she wandered. For almost a year she wandered with a great song of hatred troubling her lips. She became deranged, an idiot, and everyone adored my mother. Certainly, her song amused them.

At last she struggled to be rid of me. Among the minerals she lay. Silently among the stones of sand she lay. There where the waters begin, like the most elemental mammal she lay. She lay down alone: a small whale. And at the impossible poise between absolute flux and accidental suspense, the most beautiful woman in the world became my mother. But as nothing is absolute nor accidental: I only exchanged equilibria: I was not particularly born.

For days I suckled on the blood of my delivery. Later she learned to ease her breasts and civilized my mouth with milk. No. I played with porpoises. No. Already there is progress. So. Not even then. Not even when beginning. Then is it the beginning not the stillness that means.

If I could eclipse the commencement of the moon. Skip the schedule. Be lunatic and always plunging. Then would I evade the agony of origin. Nor would I suffer an initiation. I would be just an actress, automatic to an action. And that must be how easy. The streets seem mine if I merge with a motion I do not determine. (The fireman slides down a pole. Yes and a siren controls him. There are no obstacle. He attaches himself to the vehicle carrying him. He follows the rules and there are rules how to approach a fire.)

But this is the matter of one step. If I pretend a paralysis am i not seeing? Am I not seeing white cranes idle tonight on the disappearing sidewalk, an empty truck tapered to a spoon that makes the sidewalk disappear, hatchet grass that punctures the pavement, careless carpentry to conceal an incomplete facade, a stairway almost destroyed? But I have reached this random excrement and already my eyes begin a building here at this place of pretended paralysis.

I AM NOT STILL AS i stand here like a phony catatonic:
　　aggressively resisting. I am not, it is not important
　　am i an impermeable membrane. This resistance
　　provokes the madness of enumeration:
　　　　I am insensible to a,b,c,d,e,f,g,—
And the gamble of elimination:
　　　　　　　　A^x, B^x, C^x—.
The energy this resistance requires is itself an
alteration of temperature, at least.
So I surrender. I surrender and I multiply:
Polyblot:

Sponge.

Now am I leaning on a lamppost with metal leaves and a foundation of
dung. Details obliterate within this lift. But I become corpuscular. I
AM SEEKING THE CAPITAL INTRODUCTION TO THE
VERY FIRST WORD OF MY MIND. I WANT TO DESTROY
IT. I KNOW THAT THE VERY LAST WORD IS NOT ME.

But I am this moment and corpuscular. I am that horizontal line
laughing at the bottom of the wall.
I might be the palace protected by the wall. But I refuse protection: I
am better laughing at the bottom of the wall.

Within this kingdom of the wall is there a king and a palace gullible
to light; gullibility to light despite the infinite opacities of active men
opaque and infinite within this kingdom of the wall.
The forced stones spread. The town begins to grow among the
bones.

My father came to sanctify my birth; to sanctify the birth of Her. He
came to name my mother, His. He came to tame my mother and to
shelter her. I am supposing.

We will stabilize the sand, he said. We will contain the waters. We will
close the sky. We will squeeze the wind, he said.
　　　　　　Build me a wall!
he said that.

He said: We will call this construction by a holy name. The syllable
almost subdued him but he mastered his invention: masterfully then he
said: The House.
My mother was His. The proud scheme of protection completely

included her. And it was only after he had protected my mother from experience that he became afraid of the experience of living with her labyrinthine illusions. Soon he seldom stayed in what he called The House.

At first such room as he created strangulated us. Then my mother began to vanish: security is not a color. Paralysis is not an exercise.

I was learning my father. My father was innocent perhaps: He wanted me to participate in his perseveration of himself: he wanted me to pursue the circle of his escape. And so I left The House and went to walk with him to what he called *the corner of The Wall.*

In that crude culmination, there where the exploitation of silence looks a cobweb, he taught me the way of The Wall.

Worship this thing, he said. Esteem this enemy of impulse. Let the wall become a sacred system for you, the fundamental lie you will believe.

Outside, inside, against, beside The Wall you will hover or hide, or climb, or penetrate, or withdraw. Whatever you choose, your deed will blunder as a dumb show on THE WALL. The absurd, insensible, arbitrary, obstacle qualities of The Wall will annihilate your mind. In this place of The Wall you will discover no necessity to act. The immoveable of your awareness is The Wall. You and what you do are optional. That is the secret, he said, that is the secret of your tragic spontaneity. Be glad you are optional, he told me. His voice was deep. His eyes were shut.

But here am I. Not there. Where am I is there where I am. Here am I. Am I there where nothing is here where nothing is NOW? *I am not here for you and I will stay there.* Now there is nothing but now which is why am I here?

    Look at the cloud on the circle.
    I am full suddenly full of light.

My father said: There shall be shadow.
    I am shining shadows on The Wall.
And my father was only a shadow. His shadow of flesh divulged me: I was an apology of bone.

Anyone is of no consequence. How am I my one?

    If I am, I am If in the middle of The Way. The Way leads neither north nor south with possibilities.
Possibilities preclude a wall.
The Way lies in between two walls.

These are the ways of first and last reality.
These are the ways of populous, foul, vertiginous, predatory, vicious,
liquidating, lavatory truth. The Way is not a transformative via, nor a
road for flight from arrival nor the rhythmic gesture of a street. The
Way reveals only the curb.

It is an intestinal trap: a trick coiled labyrinthine and gutteral. I am in
the middle of the way.

I am in the middle of a dirty line squeezed by bricks of the wall
precluding possibility. But I am not if I am in the middle clearly. If I am
clearly then am I in the way of nothing.

But I am not alive nor dead.

I am not alive nor dead nor gray nor anything absolute but I am
black. That may mean gamma rays or brown or turd is another word
that may mean brown inside this intestinal trap. Brown may mean
negro. Negro may mean nothing. I am in the middle of delusion. I am
in the way of nothing. But I am in the way.

My father loved the delusion he sired. The fundamental dream of my
mother, her unnatural ignorance refreshed him and he surrounded
her with new unnecessaries; things that do not matter, have no matter
like The Wall. He gave to her. He gave of himself to her. He gave gold
to her. He told her stories of herself. He told her the myth of the
mirror. He made her the mirror of myth. He said to my mother many
nouns. He said face and sky and ear and emerald and eye, but then he
said grass. He said she was grass.

My mother wondered what she was. And so he opened the house.
He gave evening to her and winter.
He gave her alternative illusions.
He gave her a glimpse of endless, enjoyable illusion.
My father opened the house with windows.

I asked my father where was grass Or is there more than my mother as a
metaphor. Around me was my mother and The Wall and the words my
father used to call her as a sound
    I asked my father is there no grass in The House

While we live in The House he said there is no grass
When you have done with living in The House then
when you leave the Wall
when you stop your self
people carry you over THE WALL and bury you under the grass

Sometimes my father said smiling at me sometimes people bury you under the grass and near an evergreen tree

I was happy to think of the burial place and I asked my father to tell me a word for my first dream

He held me on his lap as he gave me the word for my dream *Cemetery* was what he whispered in my ear.

I would like to live in that cemetery of trees and grass but he told me I must go with him struggling for survival until I finally have done with living in The House

Then will I be taken to the cemetery And this my father called A Promise

gulls fly along a shoulder
I am baffled by
your neck concealing
flight

It does not do to say it. And I would not but I cannot do. You will not let me more than words. I wish that this word were less than. I. I will to be more than this word. You will laughing let me try. For example, flight.

Three million molecules and marrow but still I will not rise and am I still. But is there that word. Desire has its sound but is there a stillness that means. There are wings between my teeth. Or my mouth consumes some cumulae fuming near my eyes striated from the hours of the day or garbanzo is a chick-pea. Still I am still.

Touch my tongue with yours.

I would swallow the limbs of your body and refuse to Write Down and disturb the magic of my engorgement

Let me more than words: I would be more than medium or limestone. I would be more than looking more than knowing more than any of these less than looking less than knowing (*words*)

On the dirt and stones between us was my hand that lay between us like a word between my eyes

On the dirt and stones between us was my hand that lay between us like another stone. Desire has no sound.

I looked the length of more than light at you away from me Things were hanging   Rosebush maid and mirror hung. Wires screws hooks and rope were there   Rope no longer green is there in that very long room

I have heard the rope of your throat
I have heard the rope in your throat ready to squeeze
me into the syntax of stone
The sound of my life is a name you may not remember
I am losing the touch of the world to a word
You must have said anything to me

Written from 1958 to 1973

Gettin Down to Get Over

Dedicated to my mother

MOMMA MOMMA MOMMA
momma momma
mammy
nanny
granny
woman
mistress
sista

luv

blackgirl
slavegirl

gal

honeychile
sweetstuff
sugar
sweetheart
baby
Baby Baby
MOMMA MOMMA
Black Momma
Black bitch
Black pussy
piecea tail
nice piecea ass

hey daddy! hey
bro!
we walk together (an')
talk together (an')
dance and *do*
(together)
dance and do/hey!
daddy!
bro!
hey!
nina nikki nonni nommo nommo

momma Black
Momma

Black Woman
Black
Female Head of Household
Black Matriarchal Matriarchy
Black Statistical
Lowlife Lowlevel Lowdown
Lowdown and *up*
to be Low-down
Black Statistical
Low Factor
Factotem
Factitious Fictitious
Figment Figuring in Lowdown Lyin
Annual Reports

Black Woman/Black
Hallelujah Saintly
patient
smilin
humble
givin thanks
for
Annual Reports and
Monthly Dole
and
Friday night
and
(*good* God!)
Monday mornin: Black and Female
martyr masochist
(A BIG WHITE LIE)
Momma Momma

What does Mothafuckin mean?
WHO'S THE MOTHAFUCKA
FUCKED MY MOMMA
messed yours over
and right now
be trippin on my starveblack
female soul

a macktruck
mothafuck
the first primordial
the paradig/digmatic
dogmatistic mothafucka who
is he?
hey!
momma momma

dry eyes on the
shy/dark/hidden/cryin Black
face
of the loneliness
the rape
the brokeup mailbox
an' no western union roses
come inside the kitchen
and no poem
take you through the whole night
and no big
Black
burly
hand
be holdin yours
to have to hold onto
no
big Black burly hand
no nommo
no Black prince
come riding from the darkness
on a beautiful black horse
no bro
no daddy

"I was sixteen when I met my father.
In a bar.
In Baltimore.
He told me who he was
and what he does.
Paid for the drinks.
I looked.
I listened.
And I left him.

It was civil
perfectly
and absolute bull
shit.
The drinks was leakin waterweak
and never got down to my knees."

hey daddy
what they been and done to you
and what you been and done
to me
to momma
momma momma
hey
sugar daddy
big daddy
sweet daddy
Black Daddy
The Original Father Divine
the everlovin
deep
tall
bad
buck
jive
cold
strut
bop
split
tight
loose
close
hot
hot
hot
sweet SWEET DADDY
WHERE YOU BEEN AND
WHEN YOU COMIN BACK TO ME
HEY
WHEN YOU COMIN BACK
TO MOMMA
momma momma

70

And Suppose He Finally Say
"Look, Baby.
I Loves Me Some
Everything about You.
Let Me Be Your Man."
That reach around the hurtin
like a dream.
And I ain never wakin up
from that one.
momma momma
momma momma

II

Consider the Queen

hand on her hip
sweat restin from
the corn/bean/greens' field
steamy under the pale/sly
suffocatin sun

Consider the Queen

she fix the cufflinks
on his Sunday shirt
and fry some chicken
bake some cake
and tell the family
"Never mine about the bossman
don' know how a human
bein spozed to act. Jus'
never mind about him.
Wash your face.
Sit down. And let
the good Lord bless this table."

Consider the Queen

her babies pullin at the nipples
pullin at the momma milk

the infant fingers gingerly
approach caress the
soft/Black/swollen/momma breast

and there
inside the mommasoft
life-spillin treasure chest
the heart
breaks

rage by grief by sorrow
weary weary
breaks
breaks quiet
silently
the weary sorrow
quiet now the furious
the adamant the broken
busted beaten down and beaten up
the beaten beaten beaten
weary heart beats
tender-steady
and the babies suck/
the seed of blood
and love glows at the
soft/Black/swollen momma breast

Consider the Queen

she works when she works
in the laundry *in jail*
in the school house *in jail*
in the office *in jail*
on the soap box *in jail*
on the desk
on the floor
on the street
on the line
at the door
lookin fine
at the head of the line
steppin sharp from behind
in the light
with a song
wearing boots
or a belt
and a gun

drinkin wine when it's time
when the long week is done
but she works when she works
in the laundry in jail
she works when she works

Consider the Queen

she sleeps when she sleeps
with the king in the kingdom
she
sleeps when she sleeps
with the wall
with whatever it is who happens
to call
with me and with you
(to survive you make
do/you explore more and more)
so she sleeps when she sleeps
a really deep sleep

Consider the Queen

a full/Black/glorious/a purple rose
aroused by the tiger breathin
beside her
a shell with the moanin
of ages inside her
a hungry one feedin the folk
what they need

Consider the Queen.

III

MOMMA MOMMA
momma momma
family face
face of the family alive
momma
mammy
momma
woman

sista
baby
luv

the house on fire/
poison waters/
earthquake/
and the air a nightmare/
turn
turn
turn around the
national gross product
growin
really gross/turn
turn
turn the pestilence away
the miserable killers
and Canarsie
Alabama
people beggin to be people
warfare on the welfare
of the folk/
hey
turn
turn away
the trickbag university/the
trickbag propaganda/
trickbag
tricklins of prosperity/of
pseudo-"status"
lynchtree necklace
on the strong
round
neck of you
my momma
momma momma
turn away
the f.b.i./the state police/the cops/
the/everyone of the
infest/incestuous investigators
into you
and Daddy/into us

hey
turn
my mother
turn
the face of history
to your own
and please be smilin
if you can
be smilin
at the family

momma momma

let the funky forecast
be the last
one we will ever
want to listen to

And Daddy see
the stars fall down
and burn a light
into the singin
darkness of your eyes
my Daddy
my Blackman
you take my body in
your arms/you use
the oil of coconuts/of trees and
flowers/fish and new fruits
from the new world
to enflame me in this otherwise
cold place
please

meanwhile
momma
momma momma
teach me how to kiss
the king within the kingdom
teach me how to t.c.b./to make do
and be
like you
teach me to survive my

momma
teach me how to hold a new life
momma
help me
turn the face of history
to your face.

PART TWO

FROM
Passion

The Morning on the Mountains

The morning on the mountains where the mist
diffuses
down into the depths of the leaves
of the ash and oak trees
trickling toward the complexion of the whole lake
cold
even though the overlooking sky
so solemnly vermilion
sub-divides/the
seething stripes as soft
as sweet as the opening
of your mouth

Current Events

He did not!
He did so!
He did not!
I'm telling you!
You lie!
Uh-unhh.
You're kidding me!
Cross my heart and hope to die!
Really?
No shit!
Yeah?
Yeah!
The What?
The Ayatollah Khomeini!
Getoutahere.
Square business!
The Who?
The Ayatollah Khomeini of Iran!
So?
So he said it!
Big deal.

That's what I'm saying:
Thursday
November 15th
1979
the headline reads:
IRAN SET TO
FREE WOMEN
AND BLACKS
Run that by, again!
Okay:
Thursday
November 15th
No! Not that part!
Just wait a second:
Thursday
November 15th
1979 and
this is the headline:
IRAN SET TO
FREE WOMEN
AND BLACKS:
See now
I told you it's a big deal!
How was I supposed to know?
Girl
you better keep up with the news!
Yeah, yeah:
I'm planning to!

Case in Point

A friend of mine who raised six daughters and
who never wrote what she regards as serious
until she
was fifty-three
tells me there is no silence peculiar
to the female

I have decided I have something to say
about female silence: so to speak
these are my 2¢ on the subject:

80

2 weeks ago I was raped for the second
time in my life the first occasion
being a whiteman and the most recent
situation being a blackman actually
head of the local NAACP

Today is 2 weeks after the fact
of that man straddling
his knees either side of my chest
his hairy arm and powerful left hand
forcing my arms and my hands over my head
flat to the pillow while he rammed
what he described as his quote big dick
unquote into my mouth
and shouted out: "D'ya want to swallow
my big dick; well, do ya?"

He was being rhetorical.
My silence was peculiar
to the female.

Newport Jazz Festival: Saratoga Springs and Especially about George Benson and everyone who was listening

We got to the point of balloons all of us
held aloft/a tender tapping at the skin
of coloring translucent
and
nothing was too deep but the incendiary/slow the rainy/
rainbow crowded surface did not keep
anybody from caring enough to undertake a random
openhanded sharing of much hefty
toke equipment/smoke
was passing by like kisses in the air
where little girls
blew bubbles
benedictory below the softly bloated
clouds

While the trumpets lifted sterling
curvilinear tonalities
to turn the leaves down low/well-
lit by glowing globes of candlelight
that man was singing
That man was singing
Baby
Baby if you come with me
I'll make you my own Dairy Queen
or if that's locked we'll find an all-night Jack-
in-the-Box steak sandwich/fried onion rings
blackcherry/strawberry/butterscotch/shake
blackcherry/strawberry/butterscotch
shake
blackcherry/strawberry/butterscotch
shake

Baby
if you come now Baby if you if you Baby if you come
now

Patricia's Poem

"Listen
after I have set the table
folded the scottowel into napkins
cooked this delicious eggplant stuffed
with bulghur wheat
then baked the whole thing under a careful
covering of mozzarella cheese
and
said my grace

don't you bring Anita Bryant/Richard
Pryor/the Justices of the Supreme Court/don't
you bring any of those people in here
to spoil my digestive processes
and ruin
my dinner

you hear?"

Letter to the Local Police

Dear Sirs:

I have been enjoying the law and order of our
community throughout the past three months since
my wife and I, our two cats, and miscellaneous
photographs of the six grandchildren belonging to
our previous neighbors (with whom we were very
close) arrived in Saratoga Springs which is clearly
prospering under your custody

Indeed, until yesterday afternoon and despite my
vigilant casting about, I have been unable to discover
a single instance of reasons for public-spirited concern,
much less complaint

You may easily appreciate, then, how it is that
I write to your office, at this date, with utmost
regret for the lamentable circumstances that force
my hand

Speaking directly to the issue of moment:

I have encountered a regular profusion of certain
unidentified roses, growing to no discernible purpose,
and according to no perceptible control, approximately
one quarter mile west of the Northway, on the southern
side

To be specific, there are practically thousands of
the aforementioned abiding in perpetual near riot
of wild behavior, indiscriminate coloring, and only
the Good Lord Himself can say what diverse soliciting
of promiscuous cross-fertilization

As I say, these roses, no matter what the apparent
background, training, tropistic tendencies, age,
or color, do not demonstrate the least inclination
toward categorization, specified allegiance, resolute
preference, consideration of the needs of others, nor
any other minimal traits of decency

May I point out that I did not assiduously seek out
this colony, as it were, and that these certain

83

unidentified roses remain open to viewing even by
children, with or without suitable supervision

(My wife asks me to append a note as regards the seasonal but
nevertheless seriously licentious
phenomenon of honeysuckle under the moon that one may
apprehend at the corner of Nelson and Main

However, I have recommended that she undertake direct
correspondence with you, as regards this: yet
another civic disturbance in our midst)

I am confident that you will devise and pursue
appropriate legal response to the roses in question
If I may aid your efforts in this respect, please
do not hesitate to call me into consultation

Respectfully yours,

Poem about Police Violence

Tell me something
what you think would happen if
everytime they kill a black boy
then we kill a cop
everytime they kill a black man
then we kill a cop

you think the accident rate would lower
subsequently?

sometimes the feeling like amaze me baby
comes back to my mouth and I am quiet
like Olympian pools from the running the
mountainous snows under the sun

sometimes thinking about the 12th House of the Cosmos
or the way your ear ensnares the tip
of my tongue or signs that I have never seen
like DANGER WOMEN WORKING

I lose consciousness of ugly bestial rabid
and repetitive affront as when they tell me

18 cops in order to subdue one man
18 strangled him to death in the ensuing scuffle (don't
you idolize the diction of the powerful: *subdue* and
scuffle my oh my) and that the murder
that the killing of Arthur Miller on a Brooklyn
street was just a "justifiable accident" again
(again)

People been having accidents all over the globe
so long like that I reckon that the only
suitable insurance is a gun
I'm saying war is not to understand or rerun
war is to be fought and won

sometimes the feeling like amaze me baby
blots it out/the bestial but
not too often

tell me something
what you think would happen if
everytime they kill a black boy
then we kill a cop
everytime they kill a black man
then we kill a cop

you think the accident rate would lower
subsequently?

Sketching in the Transcendental

Through the long night the long trucks running the road

The wind in the white pines does not ululate like
that

Nor do the boreal meadowlands the mesopotamia
of the spirit does not sing

the song of the long trucks

The spirit differs
from a truck

a helluva lot

A Poem about Intelligence for My Brothers and Sisters

A few years back and they told me Black
means a hole where other folks
got brain/it was like the cells in the heads
of Black children was out to every hour on the hour naps
Scientists called the phenomenon the Notorious
Jensen Lapse, remember?
Anyway I was thinking
about how to devise
a test for the wise
like a Stanford-Binet
for the C.I.A.
you know?
Take Einstein
being the most the unquestionable the outstanding
the maximal mind of the century
right
And I'm struggling against this lapse leftover
from my Black childhood to fathom why
anybody should say so:
$E = mc\ squared$?
I try that on this old lady live on my block:
She sweeping away Saturday night from the stoop
and mad as can be because some absolute
jackass have left a kingsize mattress where
she have to sweep around it stains and all she
don't want to know nothing about in the first place
"Mrs. Johnson!" I say, leaning on the gate
between us: "What you think about somebody come up
with an E equals $M\ C\ 2$?"
"How you doin," she answer me, sideways, like she don't
want to let on she know I ain
combed my hair yet and here it is
Sunday morning but still I have the nerve
to be bothering serious work with these crazy
questions about
"E equals what you say again, dear?"
Then I tell her, "Well
also this same guy? I think

he was undisputed Father of the Atom Bomb!"
"That right." She mumbles or grumbles, not too politely
"And dint remember to wear socks when he put on
his shoes!" I add on (getting desperate)
at which point Mrs. Johnson take herself and her broom
a very big step down the stoop away from me
"And never did nothing for nobody in particular
lessen it was a committee
and
used to say, 'What time is it?'
and
you'd say, 'Six o'clock.'
and
he'd say, 'Day or night?'
and
and he never made nobody a cup a tea
in his whole brilliant life!"
"and
(my voice rises slightly)
and
he dint never boogie neither: never!"

"Well," say Mrs. Johnson, "Well, honey,
I do guess
that's genius for you."

1977: Poem for Mrs. Fannie Lou Hamer

You used to say, "June?
Honey when you come down here you
supposed to stay with me. Where
else?"
Meanin home
against the beer the shotguns and the
point of view of whitemen don'
never see Black anybodies without
some violent itch start up.
                    The ones who
said, "No Nigga's Votin in This Town . . .

lessen it be feet first to the booth"
Then jailed you
beat you brutal
bloody/battered/beat
you blue beyond the feeling
of the terrible

And failed to stop you.
Only God could but He
wouldn't stop
you
fortress from self-
pity

Humble as a woman anywhere
I remember finding you inside the laundromat
in Ruleville

> lion spine relaxed/hell
> what's the point to courage
> when you washin clothes?

But that took courage

> just to sit there/target
> to the killers lookin
> for your singin face
> perspirey through the rinse
> and spin

and later
you stood mighty in the door on James Street
loud callin:

> "BULLETS OR NO BULLETS!
> THE FOOD IS COOKED
> AN' GETTIN COLD!"

We ate
A family tremulous but fortified
by turnips/okra/handpicked
like the lilies

filled to the very living
full
one solid gospel
> (*sanctified*)

88

one gospel
                    (*peace*)

one full Black lily
luminescent
in a homemade field

of love

Poem for South African Women

*Commemoration of the 40,000 women and children
who, August 9, 1956, presented themselves in bodily
protest against the "dompass" in the capital of
apartheid. Presented at The United Nations, August 9,
1978.*

Our own shadows disappear as the feet of thousands
by the tens of thousands pound the fallow land
into new dust that
rising like a marvelous pollen will be
fertile
even as the first woman whispering
imagination to the trees around her made
for righteous fruit
from such deliberate defense of life
as no other still
will claim inferior to any other safety
in the world

The whispers too they
intimate to the inmost ear of every spirit
now aroused they
carousing in ferocious affirmation
of all peaceable and loving amplitude
sound a certainly unbounded heat
from a baptismal smoke where yes
there will be fire

And the babies cease alarm as mothers
raising arms
and heart high as the stars so far unseen

nevertheless hurl into the universe
a moving force
irreversible as light years
traveling to the open
eye

And who will join this standing up
and the ones who stood without sweet company
will sing and sing
back into the mountains and
if necessary
even under the sea

we are the ones we have been waiting for

Unemployment Monologue

You can call me Herbie Jr. or Ashamah
Kazaam. It don' matter much. The thing
is you don' wan' my name you
wanna mug shot
young
Black
male
who scares you chickenshit just
standin on the street just lookin
at you pass me by.
But I ain doin nothing I ain goin nowhere an
you
know it an
if you call me "Herbie" I don' mind
or "Junior"/that's all right
or "Ashamah Kazaam"/that's cool.
I say it don' really matter much ·
and then again/see
I may call you sweetmeat

I may call you tightass I might
one night I might break the windows
of the house you live in/I
might get tight and take your

wallet outasight/I might
hide out in the park to chase
you in the dark/etcetera/it
don' matter/I
may stay in school or quit
and I say
it
don' matter much
you wanna mug shot
and the way I feel about it/well
so what?

you got it!

A Song of Sojourner Truth
Dedicated to Bernice Reagon

The trolley cars was rollin and the passengers all white
when Sojourner just decided it was time to take a seat
The trolley cars was rollin and the passengers all white
When Sojourner decided it was time to take a seat
It was time she felt to rest a while and ease up
on her feet
So Sojourner put her hand out
tried to flag the trolley down
So Sojourner put her hand out
for the trolley crossin town
And the driver did not see her
the conductor would not stop
But Sojourner yelled, "It's me!"
And put her body on the track
"It's me!" she yelled, "And yes,
I walked here but I ain walkin back!"
The trolley car conductor and the driver was afraid
to roll right over her and leave her lying dead
So they opened up the car and Sojourner took a seat
So Sojourner sat to rest a while and eased up on her feet

REFRAIN:
Sojourner had to be just crazy
tellin all that kinda truth

I say she musta been plain crazy
plus they say she was uncouth
talkin loud to any crowd
talkin bad insteada sad
She just had to be plain crazy
talkin all that kinda truth

If she had somewhere to go she said
I'll ride
If she had somewhere to go she said
I'll ride
jim crow or no
she said *I'll go*
just like the lady
that she was in all the knowing darkness
of her pride
she said *I'll ride*
she said *I'll talk*
she said *A Righteous Mouth*
ain nothin you should hide
she said she'd ride
just like the lady
that she was in all the knowing darkness
of her pride
she said *I'll ride*

They said she's Black and ugly and they said she's
really rough
They said if you treat her like a dog
well that'll be plenty good enough
And Sojourner said
I'll ride
And Sojourner said
I'll go
I'm a woman and this hell has made me tough
(Thank God!)
This hell has made me tough
I'm a strong Black woman
and Thank God!

REFRAIN:
Sojourner had to be just crazy
tellin all that kinda truth

92

I say she musta been plain crazy
plus they say she was uncouth
talking loud to any crowd
talkin bad insteada sad
She just had to be plain crazy
talkin all that kinda truth

Alla Tha's All Right, but

Somebody come and carry me into a seven-day kiss
I can' use no historic no national no family bliss
I need an absolutely one to one a seven-day kiss

I can read the daily papers
I can even make a speech
But the news is stuff that tapers
down to salt poured in the breach

I been scheming about my people I been scheming about sex
I been dreaming about Africa and nightmaring Oedipus the Rex
But what I need is quite specific
terrifying rough stuff and terrific

I need an absolutely one to one a seven-day kiss
I can' use no more historic no national no bona fide family bliss
Somebody come and carry me into a seven-day kiss
Somebody come on
Somebody come on and carry me
over there!

Free Flight

Nothing fills me up at night
I fall asleep for one or two hours then
up again my gut
alarms
I must arise
and wandering into the refrigerator
think about evaporated milk homemade vanilla ice cream
cherry pie hot from the oven with Something Like Vermont

Cheddar Cheese disintegrating luscious
on the top while
mildly
I devour almonds and raisins mixed to mathematical
criteria or celery or my very own sweet and sour snack
composed of brie peanut butter honey and
a minuscule slice of party size salami
on a single whole wheat cracker *no salt added*
or I read Cesar Vallejo/Gabriela Mistral/last year's
complete anthology or
I might begin another list of things to do
that starts with toilet paper and
I notice that I never jot down fresh
strawberry shortcake: never
even though fresh strawberry shortcake shoots down
raisins and almonds 6 to nothing
effortlessly
effortlessly
is this poem on my list?
light bulbs lemons envelopes ballpoint refill
post office and zucchini
oranges no
it's not
I guess that means I just forgot
walking my dog around the block leads
to a space in my mind where
during the newspaper strike questions
sizzle through suddenly like
Is there an earthquake down in Ecuador?
Did a TWA supersaver flight to San Francisco
land in Philadelphia instead
or
whatever happened to human rights
in Washington D.C.? Or what about downward destabilization
of the consumer price index
and I was in this school P.S. Tum-Ta-Tum and time came
for me to leave but
No! I couldn't leave: The Rule was anybody leaving
the premises without having taught somebody something
valuable would be henceforth proscribed from the
premises would be forever null and void/dull and
vilified well

I had stood in front of 40 to 50 students running my
mouth and I had been generous with deceitful smiles/soft-
spoken and pseudo-gentile wiles if and when forced
into discourse amongst such adults as constitutes
the regular treacheries of On The Job Behavior
ON THE JOB BEHAVIOR
is this poem on that list
polish shoes file nails coordinate tops and bottoms
lipstick control no
screaming I'm bored because
this is whoring away the hours of god's creation
pay attention to your eyes your hands the twilight
sky in the institutional big windows
no
I did not presume I was not so bold as to put this
poem on that list
then at the end of the class this boy gives me Mahler's 9th
symphony the double album listen
to it let it seep into you he
says transcendental love
he says
I think naw
I been angry all day long/nobody did the assignment
I am not prepared
I am not prepared for so much grace
the catapulting music of surprise that makes me
hideaway my face
nothing fills me up at night
yesterday the houseguest left a brown
towel in the bathroom for tonight
I set out a blue one and
an off-white washcloth seriously
I don't need no houseguest
I don't need no towels/lovers
I just need a dog

Maybe I'm kidding

Maybe I need a woman
a woman be so well you know so wifelike
so more or less motherly so listening so much
the universal skin you love to touch and who the
closer she gets to you the better she looks to me/somebody

say yes and make me laugh and tell me she know she
been there she spit bullets at my enemies she say you
need to sail around Alaska fuck it all try this new
cerebral tea and take a long bath

Maybe I need a man
a man be so well you know so manly so lifelike
so more or less virile so sure so much the deep
voice of opinion and the shoulders like a window
seat and cheeks so closely shaven by a twin-edged
razor blade no oily hair and no dandruff besides/
somebody say yes and make
me laugh and tell me he know he been there he spit
bullets at my enemies he say you need to sail around
Alaska fuck it all and take a long bath

lah-ti-dah and lah-ti-dum
what's this socialized obsession with the bathtub

Maybe I just need to love myself myself
(anyhow I'm more familiar with the subject)
Maybe when my cousin tells me you remind me
of a woman past her prime maybe I need
to hustle my cousin into a hammerlock
position make her cry out uncle and
I'm sorry
Maybe when I feel this horrible
inclination to kiss folks I despise
because the party's like that
an occasion to be kissing people
you despise maybe I should tell them kindly
kiss my

Maybe when I wake up in the middle of the night
I should go downstairs
dump the refrigerator contents on the floor
and stand there in the middle of the spilled milk
and the wasted butter spread beneath my dirty feet
writing poems
writing poems
maybe I just need to love myself myself and
anyway
I'm working on it

Letter to My Friend the Poet
Ntozake Shange

Just back from Minnesota/North Dakota
All my clothes into the laundry or
dry cleaners before I leave
again
for Oregon then California
and my agent calls to say your business
manager is sending me
a Christmas present
from you
by messenger
within the next two hours: will
I be home?

Jesus Christ (I think) getting nervous
about two hours housebound
under the circumstances
maybe
one of us
better slow down!

En Passant

A white man tells me he told a white woman

You need to be fucked to death
You need a Black man

She said: What would my family say?

I say the same thing: What would my family
say
about that?

A Short Note to My Very Critical and Well-Beloved Friends and Comrades

First they said I was too light
Then they said I was too dark
Then they said I was too different
Then they said I was too much the same
Then they said I was too young
Then they said I was too old
Then they said I was too interracial
Then they said I was too much a nationalist
Then they said I was too silly
Then they said I was too angry
Then they said I was too idealistic
Then they said I was too confusing altogether:
Make up your mind! They said. Are you militant
or sweet? Are you vegetarian or meat? Are you straight
or are you gay?

And I said, Hey! It's not about *my* mind.

Rape Is Not a Poem

1
One day she saw them coming into the garden
where the flowers live.
They
found the colors beautiful and
they discovered the sweet smell
that the flowers held
so
they stamped upon and tore apart
the garden
just because (they said)
those flowers?
They were asking for it.

98

2

I let him into the house to say hello.
"Hello," he said.
"Hello," I said.
"How're you?" he asked me.
"Not bad," I told him.
"You look great," he smiled.
"Thanks; I've been busy: I am busy."
"Well, I guess I'll be heading out, again,"
he said.
"Okay," I answered and, "Take care," I said.
"I'm gonna do just that," he said.
"No!" I said: "No! Please don't. Please
leave me alone. Now. No. Please!" I said.
"I'm leaving," he laughed: "I'm leaving you
alone; I'm going now!"
"No!" I cried: "No. Please don't do this to me!"
But he was not talking anymore and there was
nothing else that I could say
to make him listen
to me.

3

And considering your contempt
And considering my hatred consequent to that
And considering the history
that leads us to this dismal place where (your arm
raised
and my eyes
lowered)
there is nothing left but the drippings
of power and
a consummate wreck of tenderness/I
want to know:
Is this what you call
Only Natural?

4

My dog will never learn the names
of stars or thorns but
fully he
encounters whatever it is

shits on the ground
then finds a fallen leaf still holding
raindrops from the day and
there he stays
a big dog
(licking at the tiny water)
delicate as he is
elsewhere
fierce

You should let him teach you how
to come down

Memo:

When I hear some woman say she
has finally decided you can spend time with
other women, I wonder what she means: Her
mother? My mother?
I've always despised my woman friends. Even
if they introduced me to a man I found
attractive I have never let them become
what you could call my intimates. Why
should I? Men are the ones with the money and
the big way with waiters and the passkey
to excitement in strange places of real
danger and the power to make things happen
like babies or war and all these great ideas
about mass magazines for members of the weaker sex
who need permission
to eat potatoes or a doctor's opinion on orgasm after death
or the latest word on what the female
executive should do, after hours, wearing
what. They must be morons: women!
Don't you think?
I guess you could say
I'm stuck in my ways
as
That Cosmopolitan Girl.

What Is This in Reference To?
or
We Must Get Together Sometime
Soon!

Hello.
I'm sorry.
I can't talk to you.
I am unavailable.
I am out of the house.
I am out of town.
I am out of the country.
I am out of my mind.
I am indisposed.
The cat has my tongue.
Please do not hang up.
I know this is frustrating
                    ridiculous
                    solipsistic
                    inconvenient
                    mechanical
                    and
                    a pain in the ass
Please listen for the beep.
When you hear the beep
please leave a message as long as you like
or better still
please leave a brief message
or better yet
state your purpose in concise
readily decipherable terms and be sure
to leave your name your number
the time
the date
the place
and a list of the secret desires underlying this conventional
even hackneyed outreach represented
by
your call.
This is your dime.
Listen for the beep. Sucker.

Poem about My Rights

Even tonight and I need to take a walk and clear
my head about this poem about why I can't
go out without changing my clothes my shoes
my body posture my gender identity my age
my status as a woman alone in the evening/
alone on the streets/alone not being the point/
the point being that I can't do what I want
to do with my own body because I am the wrong
sex the wrong age the wrong skin and
suppose it was not here in the city but down on the beach/
or far into the woods and I wanted to go
there by myself thinking about God/or thinking
about children or thinking about the world/all of it
disclosed by the stars and the silence:
I could not go and I could not think and I could not
stay there
alone
as I need to be
alone because I can't do what I want to do with my own
body and
who in the hell set things up
like this
and in France they say if the guy penetrates
but does not ejaculate then he did not rape me
and if after stabbing him if after screams if
after begging the bastard and if even after smashing
a hammer to his head if even after that if he
and his buddies fuck me after that
then I consented and there was
no rape because finally you understand finally
they fucked me over because I was wrong I was
wrong again to be me being me where I was/wrong
to be who I am
which is exactly like South Africa
penetrating into Namibia penetrating into
Angola and does that mean I mean how do you know if
Pretoria ejaculates what will the evidence look like the
proof of the monster jackboot ejaculation on Blackland
and if
after Namibia and if after Angola and if after Zimbabwe

102

and if after all of my kinsmen and women resist even to
self-immolation of the villages and if after that
we lose nevertheless what will the big boys say will they
claim my consent:
Do You Follow Me: We are the wrong people of
the wrong skin on the wrong continent and what
in the hell is everybody being reasonable about
and according to the *Times* this week
back in 1966 the C.I.A. decided that they had this problem
and the problem was a man named Nkrumah so they
killed him and before that it was Patrice Lumumba
and before that it was my father on the campus
of my Ivy League school and my father afraid
to walk into the cafeteria because he said he
was wrong the wrong age the wrong skin the wrong
gender identity and he was paying my tuition and
before that
it was my father saying I was wrong saying that
I should have been a boy because he wanted one/a
boy and that I should have been lighter skinned and
that I should have had straighter hair and that
I should not be so boy crazy but instead I should
just be one/a boy and before that
it was my mother pleading plastic surgery for
my nose and braces for my teeth and telling me
to let the books loose to let them loose in other
words
I am very familiar with the problems of the C.I.A.
and the problems of South Africa and the problems
of Exxon Corporation and the problems of white
America in general and the problems of the teachers
and the preachers and the F.B.I. and the social
workers and my particular Mom and Dad/I am very
familiar with the problems because the problems
turn out to be
me
I am the history of rape
I am the history of the rejection of who I am
I am the history of the terrorized incarceration of
my self
I am the history of battery assault and limitless
armies against whatever I want to do with my mind

and my body and my soul and
whether it's about walking out at night
or whether it's about the love that I feel or
whether it's about the sanctity of my vagina or
the sanctity of my national boundaries
or the sanctity of my leaders or the sanctity
of each and every desire
that I know from my personal and idiosyncratic
and indisputably single and singular heart
I have been raped
be-
cause I have been wrong the wrong sex the wrong age
the wrong skin the wrong nose the wrong hair the
wrong need the wrong dream the wrong geographic
the wrong sartorial I
I have been the meaning of rape
I have been the problem everyone seeks to
eliminate by forced
penetration with or without the evidence of slime and/
but let this be unmistakable this poem
is not consent I do not consent
to my mother to my father to the teachers to
the F.B.I. to South Africa to Bedford-Stuy
to Park Avenue to American Airlines to the hardon
idlers on the corners to the sneaky creeps in
cars
I am not wrong: Wrong is not my name
My name is my own my own my own
and I can't tell you who the hell set things up like this
but I can tell you that from now on my resistance
my simple and daily and nightly self-determination
may very well cost you your life

Grand Army Plaza
For Ethelbert

Why would anybody build a monument to civil war?

The tall man and myself tonight
we will not sleep together

we may not
either one of us
sleep
in any case
the differential between friend and lover
is a problem
definitions curse
as *nowadays we're friends*
or
we were lovers once
while
overarching the fastidious the starlit
dust
that softens space between us
is the history that bleeds
through shirt and blouse
alike

the stain of skin on stone

But on this hard ground curved by memories
of union and disunion and of brothers dead
by the familiar hand
how do we face to face a man
a woman
interpenetrated
free
and reaching still toward the kiss that will
not suffocate?

We are not survivors of a civil war

We survive our love
because we go on

loving

PART THREE

FROM
Living Room

From Sea to Shining Sea

1
Natural order is being restored
Natural order means you take a pomegranate
that encapsulated plastic looking orb complete
with its little top/a childproof cap that you can
neither twist nor turn
and you keep the pomegranate stacked inside a wobbly
pyramid composed by 103 additional pomegranates
next to a sign saying 89 cents
each

Natural order is being restored
Natural order does not mean a pomegranate
split open to the seeds sucked by the tongue and lips
while teeth release the succulent sounds
of its voluptuous disintegration

The natural order is not about a good time
This is not a good time to be against
the natural order

　　　　　*　　*　　*　　*

*"Those Black bitches tore it up! Yakkety
yakkety complain complaints couldn't see
no further than they got to have this
they got to have that they got to have
my job, Jack: my job!"*

*"To me it was Black men laid us wide open for the cut.
Busy telling us to go home. Sit tight.
Be sweet. So busy hanging tail and chasing
tail they didn't have no time to take a good
look at the real deal."*

*"Those macho bastards! They would rather blow
the whole thing up than give a little: It was
vote for spite: vote white for spite!"*

*"Fucken feminists turned themselves into bulldagger
dykes and scared the shit out of decent
smalltown people: That's what happened."*

"Now I don't even like niggers but there they were
chewing into the middle of my paycheck
and not me but a lot of other white people
just got sick of it, sick of carrying
the niggers."

"Old men run the government: You think that's
their problem?
Everyone of them is old and my parents and the old
people get out big numbers of them, voting for the dead"

"He's eighteen just like all the rest.
Only thing he wants is a girl and a stereo
and hanging out hanging out. What
does he care about the country? What
did he care?"

Pomegranates 89¢ each

2
Frozen cans of orange juice.
Pre-washed spinach.
Onions by the bag.
Fresh pineapple with a printed
message from the import company.
Cherry tomatoes by the box.
Scallions rubberbanded by the bunch.
Frozen cans of orange juice.
Napkins available.
No credit please.

3
This is not such a hot
time for you or for me.

4
Natural order is being restored.
Designer jeans will be replaced by the designer
of the jeans.
Music will be replaced by reproduction
of the music.
Food will be replaced by information.
Above all the flag is being replaced by the flag.

110

5

This was not a good time to be gay

Shortly before midnight a Wednesday
massacre felled eight homosexual Americans
and killed two: One man was on his way
to a delicatessen and the other
on his way to a drink. Using an Israeli
submachine gun the killer fired into the crowd
later telling police about the serpent in the garden
of his bloody heart, and so forth

This was not a good time to be Black

Yesterday the Senate passed an anti-busing
rider and this morning the next head
of the Senate Judiciary said he would work
to repeal the Voter Registration
Act and this afternoon the Greensboro
jury fully acquitted members of the Klan
and the American Nazi party in the murder
of 5 citizens and in Youngstown Ohio and in
Chattanooga
Tennessee and in Brooklyn and in Miami
and in Salt Lake City and in Portland Oregon
and in Detroit Michigan
and in Los Angeles and in Buffalo
Black American women and men
were murdered and the hearts
of two of the victims were carved
from the bodies of the victims, etcetera

This was not a good time to be old

Streamliner plans for the Federal Budget
include elimination of Social Security
as it exists; and similarly Medicare and Medicaid
face severe reevaluation, among other things.

This was not a good time to be young

Streamliner plans also include elimination
of the Office of Education and the military
draft becomes a drastic concern as the national
leadership boasts that this country will no longer
be bullied and blackmailed by wars for liberation
or wars
for independence elsewhere on the planet, and the like.

This was not a good time to be a pomegranate ripening on a tree

This was not a good time to be a child

Suicide rates among the young reached
alltime highs as the incidence of child
abuse and sexual abuse
rose dramatically across the nation.
In Atlanta Georgia at least twenty-eight Black
children have been murdered, with
several more missing and all of them feared dead, or
something of the sort.

This was not a good time to be without a job

Unemployment Compensation and the minimum
wage have been identified as programs
that plague the poor and the young
who really require different incentives
towards initiative/pluck and so forth

This was not a good time to have a job

Promising to preserve traditional
values of freedom, the new administration
intends to remove safety regulations
that interfere
with productivity potential, etcetera.

This was not a good time to be a woman

Pursuing the theme of traditional values of freedom
the new leadership has pledged its
opposition to the Equal Rights Amendment
that would in the words of the President-elect
only throw the weaker sex into a vulnerable
position among mischievous men, and the like.

This was not a good time to live in Queens

Trucks carrying explosive nuclear wastes will
exit from the Long Island Expressway and then
travel through residential streets of Queens
en route to the 59th Street Bridge, and so on.

This was not a good time to live in Arkansas

Occasional explosions caused by mystery
nuclear missiles have been cited
as cause for local alarm, among
other things.

This was not a good time to live in Grand Forks North Dakota

Given the presence of a United States nuclear
missile base in Grand Forks North Dakota
the non-military residents of the area feel
that they are living only a day by day distance
from certain
annihilation, etcetera.

This was not a good time to be married.

The Pope has issued directives concerning
lust that make for difficult interaction
between otherwise interested parties

This was not a good time not to be married.
This was not a good time to buy a house
at 18% interest.
This was not a good time to rent housing
on a completely decontrolled
rental market.
This was not a good time to be a Jew
when the national Klan agenda targets
Jews as well as Blacks among its
enemies of the purity of the people
This was not a good time to be a tree
This was not a good time to be a river
This was not a good time to be found with a gun
This was not a good time to be found without one
This was not a good time to be gay
This was not a good time to be Black

This was not a good time to be a pomegranate
or an orange
This was not a good time to be against
the natural order

—Wait a minute—

6
Sucked by the tongue and the lips
while the teeth release the succulence
of all voluptuous disintegration
I am turning under the trees
I am trailing blood into the rivers
I am walking loud along the streets
I am digging my nails and my heels into the land
I am opening my mouth
I am just about to touch the pomegranates
piled up precarious

7
This is a good time
This is the best time
This is the only time to come together

Fractious
Kicking
Spilling
Burly
Whirling
Raucous
Messy

Free

Exploding like the seeds of a natural disorder.

Des Moines Iowa Rap

So his wife and his daughters could qualify
Lester Williams told the people he was gonna try suicide:
suicide
He promised the papers he would definitely try
so his wife and his babies could qualify for welfare

in the new year.
Welfare.
In the new year.

I wanna job so bad I can taste it I won't waste it
Wanna job so bad

36 years old and home from the Navy
Take my blood, he said, and my bones, he said,
for the meat and the gravy/I'm a vet from the Navy!
Take my meat. Take my bones.
I'm a blood, he said.

Tried suicide. Tried suicide.

Lester Williams made the offer and the offer made news
Wasn't all that much to dispute and confuse
Wouldn't hide in no closet and under no bed
Said he'd straightaway shoot himself dead instead
Like a man
Like a natural man
Like a natural man wanna job so bad he
can taste it
he can taste it

Took the wife in his arms. Held the children in his heart.
Took the gun from his belt. Held the gun to his head.
Like a man.
Like a natural man.
Like a natural man wanna job so bad gotta waste it.
Gotta waste it.

Tried Suicide.
Tried Suicide.

First Poem from Nicaragua Libre:
teotecacinte

Can you say Teotecacinte?
Can you say it,
Teotecacinte?

Into the dirt she fell
she blew up the shell
fell into the dirt the artillery
shell blew up the girl
crouching near to the well of the little house
with the cool roof thatched on the slant
the little girl of the little house fell
beside the well unfinished for water
when that mortar
shattered the dirt under her barefeet
and scattered pieces of her four
year old anatomy
into the yard dust and up
among the lower branches of a short tree

Can you say it?

That is two and a half inches of her scalp there
with the soft hairs stiffening
in the grass

Teotecacinte
Can you say it,
Teotecacinte?

Can you say it?

from Nicaragua Libre:
photograph of managua

The man is not cute.
The man is not ugly.
The man is teaching himself
to read.
He sits in a kitchen chair
under a banana tree.
He holds the newspaper.
He tracks each word with a finger
and opens his mouth to the sound.
Next to the chair the old V-Z rifle
leans at the ready.

His wife chases a baby pig with a homemade
broom and then she chases her daughter running
behind the baby pig.
His neighbor washes up with water from the barrel
after work.
The dirt floor of his house has been swept.
The dirt around the chair where he sits
has been swept.
He has swept the dirt twice.
The dirt is clean.
The dirt is his dirt.
The man is not cute.
The man is not ugly.
The man is teaching himself
to read.

Problems of Translation: Problems of Language

Dedicated to Myriam Díaz-Diocaretz

1
I turn to my Rand McNally Atlas.
Europe appears right after the Map of the World.
All of Italy can be seen page 9.
Half of Chile page 29.
I take out my ruler.
In global perspective Italy
amounts to less than half an inch.
Chile measures more than an inch and a quarter
of an inch.
Aproximately
Chile is as long as China
is wide:
Back to the Atlas:
Chunk of China page 17.
All of France page 5: As we say in New York:
Who do France and Italy know
at Rand McNally?

117

2

I see the four mountains in Chile higher
than any mountain of North America.
I see Ojos del Salado the highest.
I see Chile unequivocal as crystal thread.
I see the Atacama Desert dry in Chile more than the rest
of the world is dry.
I see Chile dissolving into water.
I do not see what keeps the blue land of Chile
out of blue water.
I do not see the hand of Pablo Neruda on the blue land.

3

As the plane flies flat to the trees
below Brazil
below Bolivia
below five thousand miles below
my Brooklyn windows
and beside the shifted Pacific waters
welled away from the Atlantic at Cape Horn
La Isla Negra that is not an island La
Isla Negra
that is not black
is stone and stone of Chile
feeding clouds to color
scale and undertake terrestial forms
of everything unspeakable.

4

In your country how
do you say copper
for my country?

5

Blood rising under the Andes and above
the Andes blood
spilling down the rock
corrupted by the amorality
of so much space
that leaves such little trace of blood
rising to the irritated skin the face
of the confession far
from home:

I confess I did not resist interrogation.
I confess that by the next day I was no longer sure
of my identity
I confess I knew the hunger.
I confess I saw the guns.
I confess I was afraid.
I confess I did not die.

6
What you Americans call a boycott
of the junta?
Who will that feed?

7
Not just the message but the sound.

8
Early morning now and I remember
corriente a la madrugada from a different
English poem,
I remember from the difficulties of the talk
an argument
athwart the wine the dinner and the dancing
meant to welcome you
you did not understand the commonplace expression
of my heart:

the truth is in the life
la verdad de la vida

Early morning:
Do you say *la mañanita*?
But then we lose
the idea of the sky uncurling to the light:

Early morning and I do not think we lose:
the rose we left behind
broken to a glass of water on the table
at the restaurant stands
even sweeter
por la mañanita

Poem on the Road; for Alice Walker

1 On the Road
Once in awhile
it's like calling home long distance but nobody
lives there anymore

2 New Hampshire
White mountains or trout
streams or rocks sharp as a fighter plane
simply afloat
above the superhighways

Almost by herself
(trying to "live free or die")
a white girl twitching white tears
unpolluted under the roar
of Pease Air Force Base immortalized
by flyboys taking out Hiroshima
but now
real interested just to take her out
anywhere at all

This is not racist

3 Brooklyn
Running imagery through the arteries of her
pictures posted up against apartheid
what does a young Black poet do?
What does a young
Black woman poet
do
after dark?

Six dollars in her backpack
carrying the streets like a solitary
sentinel possessed by visions
of new arms new
partners

what does she do?

What does the Black man
in his early thirties
in a bomber jacket
what does the Black man do about the poet
when he sees her?
After he took the six
dollars
After he punched her
down
After he pushed
After he punctured her lungs with his knife
After the Black man
in his early thirties
in a bomber jacket
After she stopped bleeding
After she stopped pleading
(*please don't hurt me*)

what was the imagery running
through the arteries of the heart
of that partner?

This is not racist

4   New Bedford

The lady wanted to have a drink
The lady wanted to have two drinks

Four men dragged the lady to the table
Two men blocked the door
All of them laughing
Four men
Two men
All of them laughing
A lot of the time the lady could not
breathe
A lot of the time the lady wanted
to lose consciousness

Six men
One lady

All of them Portuguese

This is a promise I am making
it here
legs spread on the pool
table of New Bedford

I am not racist

I am raising my knife
to carve out the heart
of no shame

5   On the Road

This is the promise
I am making it here on the road
of my country

I am raising my knife
to carve out the heart
of no shame

The very next move is not mine

A Song for Soweto

At the throat of Soweto
a devil language falls
slashing
claw syllables to shred and leave
raw
the tongue of the young
girl
learning to sing
her own name

Where she would say
water
They would teach her to cry
blood

Where she would save
                              grass
They would teach her to crave
                              crawling into the
                              grave
Where she would praise
                              father
They would teach her to pray
                              somebody please
                              do not take him
                              away
Where she would kiss with her mouth
                              my homeland
They would teach her to swallow
                              this dust

But words live in the spirit of her face and that
sound will no longer yield to imperial erase

Where they would draw
                              blood
She will drink
                    water
Where they would deepen
                              the grave
She will conjure up
                    grass
Where they would take
                              father and family away
She will stand
                    under the sun/she will stay
Where they would teach her to swallow
                              this dust
She will kiss with her mouth
                              my homeland
and stay
with the song of Soweto

stay
with the song of Soweto

Song of the Law Abiding Citizen

so hot so hot so hot so what
so hot so what so hot so hot

They made a mistake
I got more than I usually take
I got food stamps food stamps I got
so many stamps in the mail
I thought maybe I should put them on sale
How lucky I am
I got food stamps: Hot damn!
I made up my mind
to be decent and kind
to let my upright character shine
I sent 10,000 food stamps
back to the President (and his beautiful wife)
and I can't pay the rent
but I sent 10,000 food stamps
back to the President (and his beautiful wife)
how lucky I am
hot damn
They made a mistake
for Chrissake
And I gave it away to the President
I thought that was legal I thought that was kind
and I can't pay the rent
but I sent 10,000 food stamps
back back back to the President

so hot so hot so hot so what
so hot so what so hot so hot

Trucks cruisin' down the avenue
carrying nuclear garbage right next to you
and it's legal
it's radioaction ridin' like a regal
load of jewels
past the bars the cruel
school house and the church and if
the trucks wipeout or crash
or even lurch too hard around a corner
we will just be goners

124

and it's legal
it's radioaction ridin' regal
through the skittery city street
and don't be jittery
because it's legal
radioaction ridin' the road

Avenue A Avenue B Avenue C Avenue D
Avenue of the Americas

so hot so hot so hot so what
so hot so what so hot so hot
so hot so hot so hot so what

October 23, 1983

The way she played the piano
    the one listening was the one taken
    the one taken was the one
        into the water/
        watching the foam
        find the beautiful boulders
        dark
        easily liquid
        and true as the stone
        of that meeting/molecular
        elements of lust
        distilled by the developing
        sound
        sorrow
        sound
        fused by the need of the fingers
        to note down
        to touch upon
        to span
        to isolate
        to pound
        to syncopate
        to sound
        sorrow

                    sound
                    among the waters
                    gathering
                    corpuscular/exquisite

constellations tuning among waves
the soul itself
pitched atonal but below
the constellations tuning among waves
the soul itself

a muscular/exquisite

matter of tactful
                    exact
                    uproarious

heart
collecting the easily dark
liquid
look
of the beautiful boulders

in that gathering
    that water

                                                            for a.b.t.

Menu

We got crispy chicken
we got frisky chicken
we got digital chicken
we got Chicken Evergreen

We got chicken salad
we got chicken with rice
we got radar chicken
we got chicken in the first degree

but we ain't got no fried chicken.

126

We got Chicken Red Light
we got drive-in chicken
we got felony chicken
we got chicken gravy

but we ain't got no fried chicken.

We got half a chicken
we got 2 chickens
we got Chicken Tylenol
we got chicken on ice

but we ain't got no fried chicken.

We got King Chicken
we got chicken a la mode
we got no-lead chicken

We got chainsaw chicken
we got chicken in a chair
we got borderline chicken
we got Chicken for the Young at Heart

We got aeresol chicken
we got Chicken Guitar

but we ain't got no fried chicken.

We got Coast Guard Chicken
we got sixpack chicken
we got Chicken Las Vegas
we got chicken to burn

but we ain't got no fried chicken.

We got 10-speed chicken
we got atomic chicken
we got chicken on tape

We got day-care chicken
we got Chicken Mascara
we got second-hand chicken

but we ain't got no fried chicken.

We got dead chicken
we got chicken on the hoof

we got open admissions chicken
we got Chicken Motel

We got astronaut chicken
we got chicken to go

We got gospel chicken
we got four-wheel drive chicken
we got chain gang chicken
we got chicken transfusions

but we ain't got no fried chicken

We got wrong turn chicken
we got rough draft chicken
we got chicken sodas
we got Chicken Deluxe

but we ain't
got
no

fried chicken.

Addenda to the Papal Bull
Dedicated to the Poet Nicanor Parra

The Pope thinks.
The Pope thinks all of the time.
The Pope thinks it is the duty of His
Holiness to think out loud.
The Pope thinks out loud.
The Pope thinks it is the duty of His
Holiness to publish His thoughts.
The Pope publishes His thoughts.
The Pope is thinking about peace.
He is in favor of peace.
The Pope is thinking about meat.
He is in favor of fish.

128

The Pope is thinking about women.
He thinks women can be acceptable.
These are the thoughts of the Pope on sex:
The Pope thinks that no sex is better than good.
The Pope thinks that good sex is better than sin.
The Pope thinks that sin happens
when sex happens when two people
want to have sex with each other.
The Pope thinks that is an example of lust.
The Pope thinks that lust is for the birds.
Marriage without sex without lust is permissible.
Remarriage is permissible only
without lackluster and lusty sex, both.
The Pope thinks that these thoughts
on peace and women and meat and sex
deserve our most obedient attention.
The Pope is thinking and thinking and thinking.
Who can deny the usefulness of His concern?

Poem for Guatemala
Dedicated to Rigoberto Manchú

(*With thanks to* Journey to the Depths, *the testimony of Rigoberto
Manchú, translated into English by Patricia Goedicke, October, 1982*)

No matter how loudly I call you the sound of your name
makes the day soft
Nothing about it sticks to my throat
Guatemala
syllables that lilt into twilight and lust
Guatemala
syllables to melt bullets

They call you Indian
They called me West Indian
You learned to speak Spanish when I did
We were thirteen
I wore shoes

129

I ate rice and peas
The beans and the rice in your pot
brought the soldiers
to hack off your arms

"Walk like that into the kitchen!
Walk like that into the clearing!
Girl with no arms!"

I had been playing the piano

Because of the beans and the rice in your pot
the soldiers arrived with an axe
to claim you guerilla
girl with no arms

An Indian is not supposed to own a pot of food
An Indian is too crude
An Indian covers herself with dirt so the cold
times will not hurt her

Cover yourself with no arms!

They buried my mother in New Jersey.
Black cars carried her there.
She wore flowers and a long dress.

Soldiers pushed into your mother
and tore out her tongue
and whipped her under a tree
and planted a fly in the bleeding
places so that worms
spread through the flesh
then the dogs
then the buzzards
then the soldiers laughing
at the family of the girl
with no arms
guerilla girl
with no arms

You go with no arms
among the jungle treacheries
You go with no arms
into the mountains hunting
revenge

I watch you
walk like that
into the kitchen
walk like that
into the clearing
girl with no arms

I am learning new syllables
of revolution

Guatemala
Guatemala
Girl with no arms

On the Real World:
Meditation #1.

5 shirts
2 blouses
3 pairs of jeans and the iron's on hot
for cotton:
I press the steam trigger to begin
with the section underneath the collar
from the inside out.
Then the sleeves. Starting with the cuffs.
Now the collar wrong way before it's right.
I'm not doing so good.
Around where the sleeve joins the shoulder looks
funny.
My hand stops startled.
New like a baby there's a howling on the rise.
I switch the shirt so that the iron reaches
the front panel easily.
That howling like a long walk by the Red
Brigades for twenty years between improbable
Chinese ravines with watercolor trees
poked into a spot as graceful as clouds
missing deliberate from a revolutionary land-
scape printed in Japan
ebbs then returns a louder howling cold

as the long walk towards the watery
limits of the whole earth blasted by the air
become tumescent in a lonely place
inhabited by the deaf or the invisible
but querulously looming victims of such speed
in spoken pain the louder howling large
as the original canvas containing that landscape
printed in Japan almost overloaded as the howling loses
even its small voice while I
bite my lips and lower my head
hard into the ferocity of that sound
dwarfing me into someone almost immaterial
as now I smell fire
and look down all the way to the shirt
pocket
skyblue and slightly burned

Poem on

the snow
nearly as soft
as the sleeping nipple
of your left breast

A Runaway Lil Bit Poem

Sometimes DeLiza get so crazy she omit
the bebop from the concrete she intimidate
the music she excruciate the whiskey she
obliterate the blow she sneeze
hypothetical at sex

Sometimes DeLiza get so crazy she abstruse
about a bar-be-cue ribs wonder-white-bread
sandwich in the car with hot sauce
make the eyes roll right to where you are
fastidious among the fried-up chicken wings

Sometimes DeLiza get so crazy she exasperate
on do they hook it up they being Ingrid
Bergman and some paranoid schizophrenic Mister
Gregory Peck-peck: Do
they hook it up?

Sometimes DeLiza get so crazy she drive
right across the water flying champagne bottles
from the bridge she last drink to close the bars she
holler kissey lips she laugh she let
you walk yourself away:

Sometimes DeLiza get so crazy!

DeLiza Questioning Perplexities:

If Dustin Hoffaman prove
a father be a better mother than a mother

If Dustin Hoffaman prove
a man be a better woman than a woman

When do she get to see
a Betterman than Hoffaman?

Poem Towards a Final Solution

In a press conference this afternoon the Secretary
of Space Development confirmed earlier reports
of a comprehensive plan nearing completion
in his Office.

Scheduled to meet with the President later
this week, Mr. Samuel B. Fierce the Third
jokingly termed the forthcoming package of proposals
"A Doozie".

The following represents a news team summary
of his remarks:

His Office will issue findings of a joint survey
of all National Parks conducted in cooperation with
the Department of the Interior in an effort to delimit
unnecessary vegetation.

His Office will recommend installation of nuclear
reactors inside low-growth residential areas of American
cities in order to encourage voluntary citizen re-
location at estimated savings to the Federal Government
of more than 2 billion dollars, yearly.

At the same time, Mr. Fierce suggested that he will
recommend
quick phasing out of Federal programs for
land reclamation
described by the Secretary at one particularly
light-hearted
moment during the press conference as
"Neanderthal nostalgia
for the little flowers that grow."

In addition, the Secretary indicated he will call
for the computation of food stamps as income so that,
for example, a legitimate Welfare recipient in Mississippi
will have exactly $8. a month as disposable cash.

Finally, Mr. Fierce alluded to a companion proposal
that will raise the rent for subsidized housing by 20%.

These various initiatives can be trusted to contribute
significantly to the President's economic goals and to
the development of more space, coast to coast. They
will furthermore establish the Office of
Space Development
as an increasingly powerful factor in budget-conscious
policymaking.

An unidentified reporter then queried the Secretary as to
whether this plan could fairly be translated as take
down the trees, tear-up the earth, evacuate the urban poor,
and let the people hang, generally speaking.

Mr. Fierce dismissed the question as a clear-cut attempt
at misleading and alarmist language deliberately obtuse
to the main objective of economic recovery for the nation.

134

Pending official release of his recommendations to
the President, the Secretary refused to comment on
the snow
falling on the stones of the cities everywhere.

Apologies to All the People in Lebanon
*Dedicated to the 600,000 Palestinian men,
women, and children
who lived in Lebanon from 1948–1983.*

I didn't know and nobody told me and what
could I do or say, anyway?

They said you shot the London Ambassador
and when that wasn't true
they said so
what
They said you shelled their northern villages
and when U.N. forces reported that was not true
because your side of the cease-fire was holding
since more than a year before
they said so
what
They said they wanted simply to carve
a 25 mile buffer zone and then
they ravaged your
water supplies your electricity your
hospitals your schools your highways and byways all
the way north to Beirut because they said this
was their quest for peace
They blew up your homes and demolished the grocery
stores and blocked the Red Cross and took away doctors
to jail and they cluster-bombed girls and boys
whose bodies
swelled purple and black into twice the original size
and tore the buttocks from a four month old baby
and then
they said this was brilliant

military accomplishment and this was done
they said in the name of self-defense they said
that is the noblest concept
of mankind isn't that obvious?
They said something about never again and then
they made close to one million human beings homeless
in less than three weeks and they killed or maimed
40,000 of your men and your women and your children

But I didn't know and nobody told me and what
could I do or say, anyway?

They said they were victims. They said you were
Arabs.
They called   your apartments and gardens   guerilla
strongholds.
They called   the screaming devastation
that they created   the rubble.
Then they told you to leave, didn't they?

Didn't you read the leaflets that they dropped
from their hotshot fighter jets?
They told you to go.
One hundred and thirty-five thousand
Palestinians in Beirut and why
didn't you take the hint?
Go!
There was the Mediterranean: You
could walk into the water and stay
there.
What was the problem?

I didn't know and nobody told me and what
could I do or say, anyway?

Yes, I did know it was the money I earned as a poet that
paid
for the bombs and the planes and the tanks
that they used to massacre your family

But I am not an evil person
The people of my country aren't so bad

You can't expect but so much
from those of us who have to pay taxes and watch
American tv

You see my point;

I'm sorry.
I really am sorry.

Another Poem About the Man

the man who brought you the garbage can
                        the graveyard
                        the grossout
                        the grimgram
                        the grubby grabbing
                        bloody blabbing nightly news
                        now brings you
                        Grenada

helicopters grating nutmeg trees
rifles shiny on the shellshocked sand
the beautiful laundry of the bombs falling into fresh air
artillery and tanks up against a halfnaked girl
and her boyfriend

another great success
brought to you
by trash delivering more trash to smash
and despoil the papaya
the breadfruit and bloodroot
shattered and bloodspattered
from freedom
rammed down the throat
of Grenada now Grenada she
no sing no more
Grenada now Grenada she
no sing no more she lose
she sky
to yankee invaders
Grenada now Grenada she
no sing no more

Poor Form

That whole way to Delphi
The children wrecked loaves of bread
smeared cheese banged each other
on the nose
and I must admit
I tried to obliterate such dread
disturbance of the dead the bother
of the beeline to the rose
the yowling of the healthy

Hoping to hear the gods
Having to wait on goats
we drove
not very fast
against the freeze that height promotes
the odds
against the living
that don't last

In bed
your hair beside my face
I do not sing
instead
I brace against the ending

Test of Atlanta 1979—

What kind of a person would kill Black children?
What kind of a person could persuade eighteen
different Black children to get into a car or
a truck or a van?
What kind of a person could kill or kidnap
these particular
Black children:

>   Edward Hope Smith, 14 years old, dead
>   Alfred James Evans, 14 years old, dead
>   Yosef Bell, 9 years old, dead
>   Milton Harvey, 14 years old, dead

Angel Lanier, 12 years old, dead
Eric Middlebrooks, 14 years old, dead
Christopher Richardson, 11 years old, dead
Aaron Wyche, 11 years old, dead
LaTanya Wilson, 7 years old, dead
Anthony B. Carter, 9 years old, dead
Earl Lee Terrell, 10 years old, dead
Clifford Jones, 13 years old, dead
Aaron Jackson, Jr., 9 years old, dead
Patrick Rogers, 16 years old, dead
Charles Stevens, 12 years old, dead
Jeffrey Lamar Mathis, 10 years old, missing
Darron Glass, 10 years old, missing
Lubie "Chuck" Geter, 14 years old, dead

What kind of a person could kill a Black child
and then kill another Black child and then
kill another Black child and then kill another
Black child and then kill another
Black child and then kill another Black
child
and stay above suspicion?
What about the police?
What about somebody Black?
What sixteen year old would say no to a cop?
What seven year old would say no thanks to me?
What is an overreaction to murder?
What kind of a person could kill a Black
child and then kill a Black child and then
kill a Black child?

What kind of a person are you?
What kind of a person am I?

What makes you so sure?

What kind of a person could save a Black child?

What kind of a people will lay down its
life for the lives of our children?

What kind of a people are we?

Relativity

It's 5 after 4 a.m. and nothing but my own
motion stirs throughout the waiting air
the rain completely purged earlier and all
day long. I could call
you now but that would join you to this
restless lying down and getting up to list
still another act I must commit
tomorrow if I ever sleep if I ever stop
sleeping long enough to act upon the space
between this comatose commotion
and the next time I can look into your
face. I hope you're laughing at the cans
of soup the house to clean the kitchen curtains
I will wash and iron
like so many other promises I make
myself: to sweep the stairs down
to the front door
and to answer every letter down to no
thanks.
     My own motion
does not satisfy tonight and later
in the daylight I'll be speeding through the streets
a secret messenger a wakeup agent walking
backwards maybe walking sideways
but for damn sure headed possibly southeast
as well as every other whichway
in your absolute
direction

Home: January 29, 1984

I can tell
because the ashtray was cleaned out
because the downstairs coconut is still full of milk
because actually nothing was left
except two shells hinged together pretty tough

140

at the joint
I can tell
because the in-house music now includes
the lying down look of gold and your shoulders
because there is no more noise in my head
because one room two hallways two flights of stairs
and the rest of northamerica remain
to be seen in this movie about why
I am trying to write this poem

                                        not a letter
                                        not a proclamation
                                        not a history

I am trying to write this poem
because I can tell
because it's way after midnight and so what
I can tell
eyes open or shut
I can tell
George Washington did not sleep
here
I can tell
it was you
I can tell
it really was
you

Nightline: September 20, 1982

"I know it's an unfortunate way to say it, but
do you think you can put this massacre
on the back burner now?"

Moving Towards Home

"Where is Abu Fadi," she wailed.
"Who will bring me my loved one?"
     New York Times 9/20/82

I do not wish to speak about the bulldozer and the
red dirt
not quite covering all of the arms and legs
Nor do I wish to speak about the nightlong screams
that reached
the observation posts where soldiers lounged about
Nor do I wish to speak about the woman who shoved
her baby
into the stranger's hands before she was led away
Nor do I wish to speak about the father whose sons
were shot
through the head while they slit his own throat before
the eyes
of his wife
Nor do I wish to speak about the army that lit continuous
flares into the darkness so that the others could see
the backs of their victims lined against the wall
Nor do I wish to speak about the piled up bodies and
the stench
that will not float
Nor do I wish to speak about the nurse again and
again raped
before they murdered her on the hospital floor
Nor do I wish to speak about the rattling bullets that
did not
halt on that keening trajectory
Nor do I wish to speak about the pounding on the
doors and
the breaking of windows and the hauling of families into
the world of the dead
I do not wish to speak about the bulldozer and the
red dirt
not quite covering all of the arms and legs
because I do not wish to speak about unspeakable events
that must follow from those who dare
"to purify" a people
those who dare

142

"to exterminate" a people
those who dare
to describe human beings as "beasts with two legs"
those who dare
"to mop up"
"to tighten the noose"
"to step up the military pressure"
"to ring around" civilian streets with tanks
those who dare
to close the universities
to abolish the press
to kill the elected representatives
of the people who refuse to be purified
those are the ones from whom we must redeem
the words of our beginning
because I need to speak about home
I need to speak about living room
where the land is not bullied and beaten into
a tombstone
I need to speak about living room
where the talk will take place in my language
I need to speak about living room
where my children will grow without horror
I need to speak about living room where the men
of my family between the ages of six and sixty-five
are not
marched into a roundup that leads to the grave
I need to talk about living room
where I can sit without grief without wailing aloud
for my loved ones
where I must not ask where is Abu Fadi
because he will be there beside me
I need to talk about living room
because I need to talk about home

I was born a Black woman
and now
I am become a Palestinian
against the relentless laughter of evil
there is less and less living room
and where are my loved ones?

It is time to make our way home.

PART FOUR

North Star
(New Poems)

North Star:

Stellar guide to freedom for African men and women making their escape from slavery

Signpost in the sky for sailors on the open sea

The Abolitionist newspaper founded by Frederick Douglass in 1847

Famine

I

Fifty or maybe just five flies eat at the chin
of that child: Thin except for the bloat
at the belly and the bulging eyes that watch or
more accurately
that stop
in the direction he expects his mother
to come from
if she returns
if she can
walk back
carrying water that anyway
may kill
whoever gets to drink it: It's
heavy:
Water for a day weighs more than the boy
by now
weighs more than anything else
on her mind
the woman who leaves him
possibly to die
while she hunts in the sand
mile after mile looking
for water
that will not boil roots even
or bones

because not even carcasses
of trees or animals
rot
anymore
anywhere

around

      II
On line
the elderly wait for the armory or
the church doors
to open
magnanimous with surplus saltine crackers
margarine and velveeta cheese
if you eat enough of the stuff
nobody wants to pay
money for
you fill up the freckling flesh
of what's left

      III
On line
the boys who deal
the girls who trick
somersault
suck
sneak
slide
steal
break for the sake of a meal
they feel
nothing at all

      IV
But we the holy roller
passers-by
we wallow among calories that glut

148

the braincells/overload
the willing gut
and stupefy
inert

Mustering meretricious rosaries
of hell-bent penitence
we disavow our power
saying:

"This is not the house of my father
There is no longer the lingering scent of the roses
grown on a mortgage
There is no more to the story of the fish that got
away

This not the land of my mother

There is no mountain becoming the breast of the earth
There is no one feeding us
according to need"

But suppose that we live on the land
of our people
Suppose we live in the houses
of our rightful lives
but we do not believe it
we do not insist on quick
redistribution
of these gifts/then
who are we
and how shall we defend
ourselves as members of what
family?

Intifada

In detention
in concentration camps

we trade stories
we take turns sharing the straw mat
or a pencil
we watch what crawls in and out
of the sand

As-Salāmm 'Alaykum

The guards do not allow the blue
woolen blanket
my family travelled far
to bring
to this crepuscular and gelid cell
where my still breathing infant son
and I
defy the purgatory implications
of a state-created hell

Wa 'Alaikum As-Salām

The village trembles from the heavy
tanks that try
to terrify the children:
Everyday
my little brother runs behind the rubble
practising the tactics of the stones
against the rock.
In January soldiers broke his fingers
one by one. Time has healed
his hands but not the fury that controls
what used to be
his heart.

Insha Ā'llāh

Close the villages
Close the clinics
Close the school
Close the house
Close the windows of the house
Kill the vegetables languishing under the sun
Kill the milk of the cows left to the swelling of pain

150

Cut the electricity
Cut the telephones
Confine the people to the people

Do Not Despair of the Mercy of Allah

Fig trees will grow and oranges
erupt from desert
holdings on which plastic
bullets (70% zinc, 20% glass, and 10%
plastic) will prove blood
soluble and fertilize the earth
where sheep will graze
and women no longer grieve and beat
their breasts
They will beat clean
fine-woven rugs outside a house
smelling of cinnamon
and nutmeg

Ahamdullilah

So says *Iman*
the teacher of peace
the shepherd on the mountain of the lamb
the teacher of peace
who will subdue the howling of the lion
so that we may kneel
as we must
five times beginning just after dawn
and ending just before dusk
in the *Ibādah*
of prayer

Allāhu Akbar
Allāhu Akbar
Allāhu Akbar

Glossary:
    As-Salāmm 'Alaykum: peace be unto you
    Wa 'Alaikum As-Salām: and peace be unto you

Insha A'llāh: as/if Allah wills it
"Do Not Despair of the Mercy of Allah": verse from *The Qur'ān*
Ahamdullilah: praise be to Allah
Iman: faith
Ibādah: worship in a ritual sense
Allāhu Akbar: Allah is the Greatest

Ghazal at Full Moon

I try to describe how this aching begins or how it began
with an obsolete coin and the obsolete head of an obsolete
    Indian.

Holding a nickel I beheld a buffalo I beheld the silver face
of a man who might be your father: A dead man: An Indian.

I thought, "Indians pray. Indian dance. But, mostly, Indians
    do not live.
In the U.S.A., we said, "The only good Indian is a dead
    Indian."

Dumb like Christopher Columbus I could not factor out the
    obvious
denominator: Guatemala/Wisconsin/Jamaica/Colorado:
    Indian.

Nicaragua and Brazil, Arizona, Illinois, North Dakota and
    New Mexico:
The Indigenous: The shining and the shadow of the eye is
    Indian.

One billion-fifty-six, five-hundred-and-thirty-seven-thousand
    people
breathing in India, Pakistan, Bangladesh: All of them Indian.

Ocho Ríos Oklahoma Las Vegas Pearl Lagoon Chicago
Bombay Panjim Liverpool Lahore Comalapa Glasgow: Indian.

From a London pub among the läger louts to Macchu Picchu
I am following an irresistible a tenuous and livid profile:
  Indian.

I find a surging latticework inside the merciless detritus of
  diaspora
We go from death to death who see any difference here from
  Indian.

The voice desiring your tongue transmits from the light of the
  clouds as it can.
Indian Indian Indian   Indian Indian Indian Indian.

Poem from Taped Testimony
in the Tradition of Bernard Goetz

I

This was not I repeat this was not a racial incident.

II

I was sitting down and it happened to me
before that I was sitting down or I was standing
up and I was by myself because of course
a lot of the time I am by myself because
I am not married or famous or super-im-
portant enough to have shadows or body-
guards so I was alone as it happens when
I was sitting down or let me retract that
I wasn't with anybody else regardless
who else was there
and I know I am not blind I could see
other people around me but the point
is that I wasn't with them I wasn't
with anybody else and like I said
it happened before two three
times it had happened that I was
sitting down or I was standing up

when one of them or one time it was
more than one I think it was two
of them anyway they just jumped
me I mean they jumped on me like
I was chump change and I know
I am not blind I could see they were
laughing at me they thought it was
funny to make me feel humiliated or I don't
know ugly or weak or really too small
to fight back so they were just laughing
at me in a way I mean you didn't
necessarily see some kind of a smile
or hear them laughing but I could feel
it like I could feel I could always
feel this shiver thing this fear take
me over when I would have to come into a room
full of them and I would be by myself
and they would just look at you know what
I mean you can't know what I mean
you're not Black

III

                    How would you know
how that feels when mostly you move through
outnumbered and you are the one doesn't
fit in doesn't look right doesn't read
right because you're not white
but you live
in this place in this city where
again and again
there you are inside but outside or off
and you're different and I would never know when
it would happen again that the talking
would stop or the talking would start
or somebody would say something
stupid or nasty to me like nigga
or honey or bitch or not say
anything at all like the drugstore on Sunday
and I was standing in line but the girl
behind the counter couldn't get it
together to say, "Yes. Can I help

you?" or anything at all she was counting
on silence to make me
disappear or beg or I don't know
what and okay I'm visiting New Hampshire
but also
I live here I mean in this country
I live here and you should have seen
the look of her eyes they were shining
I know I am not blind and she wanted
to make believe me this irreducible this me
into a no-count what you gone do about
it/zip

        IV
So one of them a policeman a long
time ago but I remember it he kicked
in the teeth of Jeffrey Underwood who
lived on my block and who had been the best
looking boy in the neighborhood and he was tall
and skinny even and kind of shy and he/
Jeffrey went up on the roof with fire
crackers I mean it was the roof of the house
of a family that knew him and they knew
Jeffrey's parents too and
my cousin told me the next morning how
this policeman asked Jeffrey to come
down so Jeffrey left the roof and came
down to the street where we lived and
then the policeman beat Jeffrey
unconscious and he/the
policeman who was one of them he kicked
Jeffrey's teeth out and I never wanted to see
Jeffrey anymore but I kept seeing
these policemen and I remember how
my cousin who was older than I was I remember how
she whispered to me, "That's what they
do to you"

        V
and the stinging of my face when some of
them my mother told me they were

Irish and when some of them shot at me
with zip guns and howled out "lil'l nigga"
I was eight years old by myself walking
with my book bag to a public school
and I remember my mother
asking me to kneel down beside her to pray
for the Irish

VI

So much later and of course this is not something
I keep on the front burner but then again
it's nothing you want to forget because
enough is enough and it has happened before
and it happens so often but when you turn around
for help or the punishment of these people
where can you go I mean I was raped six
years ago by one of them who was good he told me
with a rifle and he raped me and his
brother was the judge in town and so forth all
of them have brothers all over town there
are so many of them everywhere you go so
either you become the routine
setup
or you have to figure out
some self-defense

VII

I was sitting down and it had happened
before that I was sitting down and I was
by myself because not one of them was
with me not one of them was cognizant
(to use a better word) of me where I
was sitting down and they filled up
the room around me and one of them
sat down to my left and another one
of them sat down beside my right fist
on the table (next to the silverware) and
I was sitting there quiet and mild-
mannered which is how I am you can
ask my neighbors you can read about

156

it in the papers everyday the papers
tell you I am quiet and mild-mannered which is
how I sat there at this table in a room
full of them and then the one to the right
of my right fist she started up about this South
African novel she was reading and she said to the one
to my left by which I mean she ignored me in the middle
and it felt like I was
not there but I was I was sitting
in my chair at that table where
she the one to my right said to the one
to my left she said, "And the writer
expects the reader to be sympathetic
to that character!" And then the
one to my left said to the one to my
right she said, "Exactly! And it's
so cheap. It's so disgusting. She (the
writer) makes her (the character)
marry not one but two Black revolutionaries!!" And
   something snapped
inside me I could see across the table
more of them just sitting there eyes
shining
and I know I am not blind
I could see them laughing at me and I went
cold because in a situation like that
you have to be cold a cold
killer or they will ridicule you
right there at the dining table and
I wanted to murder
I wanted them to hurt and bleed I wanted
them to leave me alone
and so I became cold I became a cold
killer and I took out my gun and
I shot the one to my right and then
I shot the one to my left and then I looked
across the table and I thought, "They
look all right," and so I shot them too
and it was self-defense I wanted
them to stop playing with me
I wanted them to know it's not cheap
or disgusting to love a Black

revolutionary and
as a matter of fact
I wanted them to know you'd
better love a Black revolutionary before she
gets the idea

that you don't

Aftermath

Morning sun heats up the young beech tree
leaves and almost lights them into fireflies

I wish I could dig up the earth to plant apples
pears or peaches on a lazy dandelion lawn

I am tired from this digging up of human bodies
no one loved enough to save from death

To Free Nelson Mandela

Every night Winnie Mandela
Every night the waters of the world
turn to the softly burning
light of the moon

Every night Winnie Mandela
Every night

Have they killed the twelve-year-old girl?
Have they hung the poet?
Have they shot down the students?
Have they splashed the clinic the house
and the faces of the children
with blood?

Every night Winnie Mandela
Every night the waters of the world
turn to the softly burning
light of the moon

They have murdered Victoria Mxenge
They have murdered her
victorious now
that the earth recoils from that crime
of her murder now
that the very dirt shudders from the falling blood
the thud of bodies fallen
into the sickening
into the thickening
crimes of apartheid

Every night
Every night Winnie Mandela

Every night Winnie Mandela
Every night the waters of the world
turn to the softly burning
light of the moon

At last the bullets boomerang
At last the artifice of exile explodes
At last no one obeys the bossman of atrocities

At last the carpenters the midwives
the miners the weavers the anonymous
housekeepers the anonymous
street sweepers
the diggers of the ditch
the sentries the scouts the ministers
the mob the pallbearers the practical
nurse
the diggers of the ditch
the banned
the tortured
the detained
the everlastingly insulted
the twelve-year-old girl and her brothers at last

the diggers of the ditch
despise the meal without grace
  the water without wine
  the trial without rights
  the work without rest
at last the diggers of the ditch
begin the living funeral
for death

Every night Winnie Mandela
Every night

Every night Winnie Mandela
Every night the waters of the world
turn to the softly burning
light of the moon

Every night Winnie Mandela
Every night

Dance: Nicaragua

NI SE RINDE NI SE VENDE
NI SE RINDE

Nicaragua
Todas las armas al pueblo
Todo el pueblo al sueño
Nicaragua Nicaragua
Todo el pueblo al sueño

Nicaragua Nicaragua
Bluefields/Estelí/Managua

Picking coffee in the morning
Playing basketball at night
Pencil manifestos under new electric light

Nicaragua
going back to Nicaragua
to the land of Sandinistas
to the land of New World vistas

GOING BACK
GOING BACK TO
Nicaragua Nicaragua
Bluefields/Estelí/Managua
going back to little Nica
not Honduras/Costa Rica
going back to little Nica

Fill my plate with rice and beans
Talk with parrots from the hushed up hills
of green
Swim beside the blown up bridges
Fish inside the bomb-sick harbors
Farm across the contra ridges
Dance with revolutionary ardor
Swim/Fish/Farm/ Dance
Nicaragua   Nicaragua

NI SE RINDE   NI SE VENDE
NI SE RINDE

nicaragua

vivir libre
vivir libre
vivir libre
o morir!

Verse for Ronald Slapjack
Who Publicly Declared, "I, Too, Am a
Contra!"

You said it.
You got that right.
Finally you told it to the people:
"I, too am a contra."
All except the "too" stuff:
How you mean that "too"?
Too compared to what/who stalks
around the planet like you do?
You the crown conniver
You the jivetime star
You the megajoint
You the program you the point
to every hotline launchpad eagle
program spying high
and spying low
for any signs of independent life (uh-oh)
Oops!
Swoop down! Pounce
and seize it,
Undercut them vital signs:
"Independent life," indeed.

"I, too, am a contra."

You got that right.
You the founding father
for the morally retarded
     the armed with butter-for-brains and truly mean
     the burn and brag
     the mercenaries
     the leftover lackies from last year's greed freak
     the do-anything-go-anywhere for the thrill
        of a little killing or
        if flexible
        a big kill

You the founding father

But still
that ain' no news
we seen the pot-rot way back
when
we seen you

        contra-dictory
        we seen you
        contra-dicted
        we seen you
        contra-factual
        we seen you
        contra-verified
        we seen you
        contra-Constitution
        we seen you
        contra-Bill-of-Rights
        we seen you
        contra-sanctuary
        we seen you
        contra-smart
        we seen you
        contra-all-intelligence
        we seen you
        contra-hospital-ship
        we seen you
        contra-heart
        we seen you
        contra-any-sign-of-independent-life

Fact is
Mister Slapjack Quack-Quack
in a happy
peaceful
law-abiding scheme of things
you jus' contra-indicated!

Poem Instead of a Columbus Day Parade

Yes Baby:

"Unrest in the Philippines":

Is it 7,000 islands
Am I 7,000 fragments from a country
Christopher Columbus
wrecked the reputation of the compass
by?

Did somebody ask an Indian
to pay for parking anywhere at all?

Yes Baby:

"Unrest in the Philippines":

My daily politics
an open hydrant pouring water
into late November rain

An Always Lei of Ginger Blossoms for the First Lady of Hawai'i: Queen Lili'uokalani

Dedicated to Philip and Diana Chang

Never mind
Even the Be-Still tree will never stop
the spirit rivers of the Koolau* mountains
nor the twisting smash surf drown

Koolau is pronounced "koe-oh-lah-ooh."

the great gong
pounded by the living
for the right to live

On your island dolphins
slope below belief
then rise in somersault or triple flip affection
for the laughter of the weary
ones who need

more than African tulips
more than bareback riding of a whale
more than Banyan roots
more than Diamond Head above their shoulders
more than mango guava sugarcane or pineapple and papaya
more than monkey pod elegance of shelter
more than the miracle revised to feed the blue and silver and
        yellow and spotted and large and small fish who receive
        bread from the fingers of a hand
more than forgive and forget about "the secret annexation
        society"

                mainlander businessmen who held you
                prisoner
                inside the Iolani Palace
                kept you
                solitary in confinement
                nine months
                minus even pencils or a piece of paper
                nine months
                before the businessmen relented
                and allowed you your guitar

more than the southern star skies
                and the delivering wild ocean swells
                that rule the separating space
                between Tahiti and the statue
                of Your Highness
                schooling Honolulu into secret conduct
                suitable for thimbleberries
                suitable for orchids
                suitable for the singing ghost of your guitar

165

On your island dolphins
slope beyond belief
then rise

On your island *(never mind)*
the weary ones throng
faithful to the great song
once again to pound
the great gong
sounds again and then
again

Something Like a Sonnet for Phillis Miracle Wheatley

Girl from the realm of birds florid and fleet
flying full feather in far or near weather
Who fell to a dollar lust coffled like meat
Captured by avarice and hate spit together
Trembling asthmatic alone on the slave block
built by a savagery travelling by carriage
viewed like a species of flaw in the livestock
A child without safety of mother or marriage

Chosen by whimsy but born to surprise
They taught you to read but you learned how to write
Begging the universe into your eyes:
They dressed you in light but you dreamed with the night.
From Africa singing of justice and grace,
Your early verse sweetens the fame of our Race.

Poem for Benjamin Franklin

Who said,
"I do not believe we shall ever have a firm peace with the Indians,
till we have well-drubbed them."

My Daddy, Mr. Franklin, my truculent
no-paunch
crack a coconut with one whack
of a handy homeowner's hammer-axe/my
Daddy, Mr. Franklin, my fastidious
first runaway from a true calypso/my
Daddy, Mr. Franklin, my Daddy give this
little girl
your glorified life story she
must read
or else
when she didn't know much better than to trust
some pontiff-politician talk about save pennies/
take a stitch in time

anyway

you the one gone out there in the lightning
with a kite?

Let me electrify the ghost
of your redoubtable achievements!

The Indians been well drubbed
The Palestinians been well drubbed

firm peace prevails
in 2 out of every 3 American bedrooms
and
on the nighttime city sidewalks
Firm peace prevails

and
underneath the hanging tree
and
moaning down at Wounded Knee
and north of Ocatál

and
east of Ilopongo
and
censored in the sandpits of an occupied West Bank
and
all around Johannesburg where boiling water in a tin can
has become a crime

Firm peace prevails
Mr. Franklin
Firm peace prevails

We been well drubbed
but
like my Daddy could have told you/my
Daddy whistling in the ghetto
of your legacy/my
Daddy could have told you after he done beat me
how I laid real low bud didn't hardly overlook to pay him
back
(big men must sleep sometime)
My Daddy/Mr. Franklin/my Daddy could have told you
firm peace ain' peace it's truce
and truce don't last
but temporarily

The Torn Sky: Lesson #1

chlorofluorocarbons
chlorofluorocarbons
chlorofluorocarbons

start at Antarctica

chlorofluorocarbons
chlorofluorocarbons
chlorofluorocarbons

168

like a Spanish speaking Afrikaner
(or
an Afrikaner speaking Spanish)

start at Antarctica

(now you're getting it)

chlorofluorocarbons
chlorofluorocarbons
chlorofluorocarbons

start at Antarctica

(to tear up the sky)

Take Them Out!

Take them out!

Rain forests of the world
only provide x amount of oxygen
for everybody including some
you don't like anyhow

Rain forests of the world
only provide x amount of refuge
for x amount of living creatures
most of which you never seen
even in the movies

Take them out!

From Alaska to Brazil you want
to keep that kind of uncontrolled
diversity in stock?

Poem for Jan

Dedicated to Jan Heller Levi

Crushed marigold or
a child's hand
crushed
the colors blurring into sunset
or royalty spelled by liquid pastel
implications of delight

Crushed marigold or
a child's hand
crushed

In what context you may ask me
For what reason
    that small flower
    that small hand
    as commonplace as lechery
    third degree burns
    or quietly contriving torture
    of a little bit of hope

To do that thing

regardless of aesthetics
regardless of some use

Crushed marigold or
a child's hand
crushed

I cannot imagine an excuse

Solidarity
For Angela Y. Davis

Even then
in the attenuated light
of the Church of le Sacre Coeur
(early evening and folk songs
on the mausoleum steps)
and armed
only with 2 instamatic cameras
(not a terrorist among us)
even there
in that Parisian downpour
four
Black women (2 of Asian 2
of African descent)
could not catch a taxi
and
I wondered what umbrella
would be big enough to stop
the shivering
of our collective impotence
up
against such negligent
assault

And I wondered
who would build that shelter
who will build and lift it
high and wide
above
such loneliness

In Paris
Dedicated to Pratibha Parmar and Shaheen Haque

I do not dare to reject the quarter moon
that perforates a clear night
sky

Adamantine above dark trees
the sliver of its lucid invitation
emulates
the willing calm of lovers
fallen
almost asleep

Between stone walls the tourist
boats float
silently electifried
under le Pont Royal

What would Louis the Fourteenth
make
of my two friends and me
our eyes as commonly tender
as the mud
our vision tempered by diaspora?

And who cares?

We stand beside the river
speaking quietly somewhere
comfortable
below the stars

At this moment
the water itself
begins to melt

Nothing
Not tears
Not even the rain
As soft as the Seine

Poem on the Second Consecutive Day of Rain

It just don't stop/flood
levels falling/if the meadow was a Tub
of Butterflies Blue Violets
and Harebells (not to mention)
Morning Glories
Foxglove
Purple Loosestrife
Indian Paint Brush
Oxeye Daisies and
Stiff Asters
at the grassy birds' nests bottom
then I'd swim the surface of this birdsong
sanctuary
on my belly looking down
and float
complacent as the quietly pointed white pine needles
in such water saturated air

But this meadow got no bottom/
base line/absolute: This meadow sucks it up:
A rich man running after money/more
rain more more
more rain

It just don't stop!

Out in the Country of My Country (Peterborough, New Hampshire)

Filling my eyes with flowers of no name
that I can call aloud: This northernmost retreat
of white pine or aching birch
of meadow mouth opening the body of a perfect land

that throws away birdsong on the rushes
of hard rain

Testing my heart with precipice and crest
accumulating timber trails or fern
beside the mica sparkling road that peaks
at mountain heights of granite situated
next to purple lilac feeling out the light
of short cold days

Choosing my mind between mosquitos and the moon
that dominates a darkness larger than the stars
close by: I (what do you suppose)
I battle with the spirits of a winterkill
that spoils the summer berries: Blunts the nipple points
of love

Chasing my face among displacements of a stream
I behold the Indian: I become the slave
again I am hunting/I am hunted in these snowy woods
again I am eagle/I am scrambling on the summit rocks
I slip I scream I soar I seek the dancing of the spirits
from the grave

A Richland County Lyric for Elizabeth Asleep

His wet nose pushing at the screen
the big dog indicates he's had enough
inside
the table oilcloth flaps beneath a cabin lamp

I let him go and follow
slowly
held by full moon on the flying ants
the flying hawk at large and silent in its odd
nocturnal drift towards mysterious emergency—

How soft it seems! The misted termination
of that hillside: (Solid black beside the easing
only human light
a mile away)

                              A forest breast/a midnight
                                 nursing of the cirrus
        clouds that lead the hawk beyond its vision
and beyond my own into the trusting evolution
of apparently pale flowers that ignite
the darkening prairie surf
like stars

The Madison Experience
Dedicated to Nellie McKay

              I
Lake Michigan
(like so much hearsay:
Who says, "lake" and who
can hold this surging body
thrust against these cities?
Who can prove the limits of original wild water
how?
But then
Lake Michigan is not the point)

              II
I am in Miami/no
Waikiki/no
It's Oxford on the definitely northern Lake
Mendota floats along with Women's
Studies/Big Ten Football
and canoes/the sailboats
tease the students and their teachers
from a coming summer's ease with beer and yoghurt

175

and next Friday night
at 6 o'clock
a rally for Soweto

III
Crayola was right:
Color this farmland green and blue
and yellow pastels
Make the barn red
Look at the silo and notice the cows
in the middle
of the University

IV
How many Black people live in Madison?
How many buffalos sleep in the park?
How many Indians came to the bar-be-cue?
When is the last time it rained?

V
Bicycles deliver urban lyrics
uphill:
hard labor habits from a hearty breakfast
for a stiff day's work on the difficult
but rolling
earth

VI
Yesterday I went out
Looking for traffic

VII
As far as I know
Sundays come and Sundays go
but there won't be no
Gay Pride March (unless somebody plans to show
by accident)

VIII
Shelling beans
snow peas/onions/hosed
down beets/ potatoes/ornamental cabbages
Planned Parenthood or fathers
for Equal Rights/whole wheat sticky
buns/potted tiger lilies/"Cheese
Curds Guaranteed to Squeak" and "What
Can One Man Do
to Stop Rape?" at The Farmers' Market
Saturdays
around the domed white Capitol Building
scrubbed clean like most
of the children fingering the flowers
and the homemade fudge

IX
7:30 A.M.
and my neighbor Bonnie
brings me a pile of still hot chocolate
chip cookies because
"They taste better like that" but
her daughter burned her forearm on the oven
and underneath my barefeet the bristling July
grass
as delicate as last October

X
Inside the always unlit hardware store
where no more than one customer per half
an hour opens or shuts the door
Mrs. Schensky mans a cash
register probably full of Rumanian jewels
that remind her of the orchids
planted all around her kitchen sink
or else those—"Well
they look like morning glories but
they grow on bushes
thousands of them—Oh, hibiscus! Do you know
hibiscus?"

I am there to buy a rubber floor mat that spells
WELCOME but that translates
into PLEASE : NO MUD

"I don't want anything to hurt you," she
declares. And so I wait
obedient
as Mrs. Schensky first removes the stapled price
tag from the floor mat
she will finally allow me
to accept
into my own two tenderly
astounded hands

                    XI
Drought around the eyes
Drought around the mouth
and words falling out like logs
from the irresistible
big trees

                    XII
Five days stretch thick skin
across the skull
of quick romance

Above the backyard mulberry tree leaves a full moon
    Not quite as high as the Himalaya Mountains
not quite as high as the rent in New York City
summons me beyond my mind into the meat and mud
of things that sing

                    XIII
The Chancellor The Mayor The County Executive
Somebody and Jesus
all played volleyball
together
and I don't remember anybody
losing it.

XIV
Who is a small burrowing mammal
head-over-heels in bona fide hog heaven
plumb full of sunlight/veal brats
and an opening heartland of surprise?

A Sonnet from the Stony Brook

Studying the shadows of my face in this white place
where tree stumps recollect a hurricane
I admire the possibilities of flight and space
without one move towards the ending of my pain.
I conspire with blackbirds light enough to fly
but grounded by the trivia of appetite
I desist decease delimit: I deny
the darling dervish from a half-forgotten night
when mouth became a word too sweet
to say aloud and body changed to right
or wrong ways to prolong new irresponsibilities of heat
new tunings of a temperature with weight and height.

For all I can remember all I know
only shadows flourish; shadows grow

A Sonnet for A.B.T.

But one of these Wednesdays everything could work
the phone and the answering machine: Your voice
despite the 65 miles that would irk
or exhaust a fainthearted lover: Your choice
of this distance this timing between us bends
things around: Illusory landmarks of longing and speed.
A full moon the flight of summer sends
to light a branch the leaves no longer need.

A top ten lyric fallen to eleven
But meaningful *(meaningful)* because the music still
invites a kind of close tight heaven
of a slowdown dance to let me kill the chill.

You know what I mean
My Love: Seen or unseen

Poem on Bell's Theorem
or Haying the Field by Quantum Mechanics

The tractor stuck between the strewn or
uncollected and the baled-up grass
mounded circles because somebody worried
about spontaneous combustion if you cubed
that igneous that throttled mass
drenched to the centermost stalk
and the farmer gone home to drink
(his son slipped from his lap since noon)
through this unpromising but slight
disaster
this intermittent and torrential rain
bringing to a halt a poor man's bare
rituals of preparation for the hushed-
up months
when green becomes an obscene
color for a discount
portable tv
                Now
it seems that water holds the land
in faulted frieze
but no stopped trucks nor turned-off key
originated here along this flooding dirt path
where I see what I may see

More likely melted glacier molecules
capricious in flirtations with an underground
magnetic tease

Or Chinese peasants killing cattle that upset
new market monetary rules
Or beaten farmers' wives who commandeer
a neighbor's car/jump-start the pickup for a get-
away from on-and-off the bottle boys
more likely these
far probabilities
making connections faster than light
compelled the man's machine to lose its energy
abandon aim
and caused the sunburned driver
just to walk himself
out of my local my mistaken sight

Poem Number Two on Bell's Theorem
or The New Physicality of Long Distance Love

There is no chance that we will fall apart
There is no chance
There are no parts.

Last Poem on Bell's Theorem
or Overriding the Local Common Sense of Causes to Effect

No:
I did not buy this sweatshirt with
        NORTH STAR
imprinted on the front
because:
        I found it on sale.
        It fit.
        I am a Minnesota hockey fan.

Look at me
and guess again.

Romance In Irony

I would risk ticks

and Rocky Mountain Spotted Fever

stop smoking

give up the car and the VCR

destabilize my bank account

floss before as well as after meals

and unilaterally disarm my telephone connection

to

other (possible) lovers

if

we could walk into the mountains then

come home again

together

But instead

I lie in bed

fingering photographs from Colorado

that conceal more than they illuminate

the hunter of the elksong or the deer.

I resent the radiator heat

that nightly rises almost musical

in a wet hot air

crescendo

or I exaggerate some not bad looking trees

that 2 or maybe 3 feet there (away from me)

and out the window

grow

oblivious above a miscellaneous

debris

(I yearn for non-negotiable abutment

to the beauty of the world)

And with the courage that the lonely or the

                              foolish keep

I set the clock

turn out the light

and do not dream and do not sleep

Trying to Capture Rapture

The point is not to pacify the soul
Or sleep through torments measuring the night
And I concede I hold no trust or goal
That, trembling, yet retains the body's light.
And I admit I hardly understand
the motions of a hand that wants a hand
Or deadlines for a love that perseveres.
But I cannot survive the blurring of the years:
Untouched, unknown, estranged and, now, alone.

And having said, "I cannot," here I do
Again declare: I will not beg for you.
And love will say, "Nobody asks you to!"
But I have died for rapture other days.
Oh, I have tried for rapture other ways!

Winter Honey

Sugar come
and sugar go
Sugar dumb
but sugar know
ain' nothin' run me for my money
nothin' sweet like winter honey

Sugar high
and sugarlow
Sugar pie
and sugar dough
Then sugar throw
a sugar fit
And sugar find
a sugar tit
But never mind
what sugar find

ain' nothin' run me for my money
nothin' sweet like winter honey

Sugar come
and please don' go
Sugar dumb
but oh-my: Oh!
Ain' nothin' run me for my money
nothin' sweet like winter honey

At Some Moment the Confidence Snaps

At some moment the confidence snaps

that tomorrow or next year or in the middle of spring

you will be

around

to run errands/drink coffee/want love/write

history

does not know about the inside snap

but this is not

historical

this is me

by myself on a quiet Friday night

not at all sure

about the future tense

of my single life

limited

by time already taking away

my arrogance

or easy postponement

of anything whatsoever

How much do I hope

that the memories of my minute

among so many strangers

will mainly taste

sweet

to the mouth of judgement

Double Standard Lifestyle Studies: #1

For example I would slit
my eyes
if I supposed your close and ravenous
inquiries might reach into a corpus
not my own

Or I would assume you would assume
Me/solitary on a gorgeous night
of tropical compulsions from the flesh
or astral incantations to the ecosystems
of my lust

But I take this call from California/
an aerogram arrives
and I watch for signals from Tibet
while you perhaps return
from Washington, D.C.

                    Baby
I guess I have trouble getting the geography
on screen

Could be monogamous monopolies
will have to wait
until some footloose wizard can identify
exact locations
on this high risk undertaking
for conventional cartographers

Or should I build implacable
my homebase
right around that millimeter where
imagination will not tempt me from the mesmerizing marvel
of your honest or deceitful
lips?

Poem for Joy
Dedicated to the Creek Tribe of North America

Dreaming
        Colorado where the whole earth rises
        marvellous high hard rock higher than the heart can
        calmly tolerate: The hawk
        swoons from its fierce precipitation
        granite in its rising opposition to the bird
        or rabbit
        Sapling leaf or stallion loose among the chasmic
        crevices dividing continental
        stretch into the small scale appetizers
        then the lifted meal
        itself

And dazed
     by snowlight settled like a glossary
     of diamonds on the difficult
     ice-bitten mountain trails that lead
     to fish rich waters

I reach
     the birthplace for the stories of your hurt
     your soft collapse
     the feelings of the flat wound of the not forgotten
                                   graves

     where neither rain nor dawn
     can resurrect the stolen pageantry the blister
     details of the taken acreage
     that scars two million memories of forest
     blueberry bush and sudden
     mushrooms sharing dirt
     with footprints tender as the hesitations
     of your hand
              who know obliteration
              who arise from the abyss
              the aboriginal
              as definite as heated through as dry
              around the eyes
              as Arizona
              the aboriginal
              as apparently inclement as invincible
              as porous
              as the desert
              the aboriginal
              from whom the mountains slide
              away
              afraid to block the day's deliverance
              into stars and cool air lonely
              for the infinite invention of avenging
                               fires

    And now the wolf
    And now the loyalty of wolves
    And now the bear
    And now the vast amusement of the bears

And now the aboriginal
And now the daughter of the tomb.

And now an only child of the dead becomes the mother
of another life,
And how shall the living sing of that
impossibility?
              She will.

Poem at the Midnight of My Life

I never thought that I would live forever:
Now I light a cigarette
surprised by pleasures lasting past
predictions from the hemorrhaging of fears
and I reflect on faces soft above my own
in love

The implications of all heated ecstasy that I have known
despite the soldier fist on broken bone
despite the small eyes shrinking flesh to stone
surround me in this tender solitude
like teenage choirs of gullibility
and guts

(How many bottles of beer will it take
to make a baby?)

I understand how nothing ever happens on a one-
plus-one equals anything predictable/
how time rolls
drunk around the curvilinear conventions
of a virgin
and eventual as passion's lapse
just peters out
indefinite

(92 bottles of beer on the wall
92 bottles of beer)

                    how sorrow brings you
to the graveside
on an afternoon of trees entirely alive

(if one of the bottles should happen to fall . . .)

the chosen focus tortured true
between a homeless woman lying frozen
on the avenue
and a flying horse or legs to carry you or race
into the hungers of a problematic
new embrace

(. . . 91 bottles of beer on the wall)

I understand the comfortable temptation of the dead:
I turn my back against the grave
and kiss again the risk of what I have
instead

The Female and the Silence of a Man
(c.f. W. B. Yeats' "Leda and the Swan")

And now she knows: The big fist shattering her face.
Above, the sky conceals the sadness of the moon.
And windows light, doors close, against all trace
of her: She falls into the violence of a woman's ruin.

How should she rise against the plunging of his lust?
She vomits out her teeth. He tears the slender legs apart.
The hairy torso of his rage destroys the soft last bastion
                              of her trust.
He lacerates her breasts. He claws and squeezes out her
    heart.

She sinks into a meadow pond of lilies and a swan.
She floats above an afternoon of music from the trees.

190

She vanishes like blood that people walk upon.
She reappears: A mad *bitch* dog that reason cannot sieze;
A fever withering the river and the crops:
A lovely girl protected by her cruel/incandescent energies.

Poem for Buddy
Dedicated to André Morgan

In that same beginning winter
when the rains strained all credulity
swallowed highways
rolled mountains of mud down
mountains
buried boundaries
left 20,000 families homeless

In that same beginning winter
of the rivers rising up
some of the people rose
organic
secretly
out loud
and irresistible

In that same beginning winter
of the gods asleep
rain
rain
rain
flood
mudslide and
the powerful at large and
lies
lies
lies
the rivers burst torrential
to attack to overcome
the limitations of all compromise

In that same beginning winter
when Duvalier and Marcos
fell into the torrents
streaming full and efflorescent out
between the blank walls and the sea
streaming aboriginal
as female

when the ku klux klan
the Duck Club and other crackpot
rah-rah
butchered Charles and Annie Goldmark
in Seattle
hung Timothy Lee
from a California weed tree
and captured two top nominations
in the State of Illinois
when Reagan reigned
from the Gulf of Sidra to the asinine appeal
of right-to-life
explosives and warmongering
cutbacks on the already alive

when the great lakes trembled
when volcanoes shook
when the desert flowers failed
when the farmers lost the land
when the Challenger blew up
when the Chairman of the Board skipped lunch

when the rain the lies lies lies
and the rain
and the rain
when the rivers burst torrential
to attack to overcome
the limitations of all compromise

from Pretoria to Port-au-Prince
from Manila to Managua
from the hanging tree for Timothy Lee
to Washington, D.C.
when the rivers burst torrential

it was then that
in Manhattan
one Black homosexual
in a gym
by himself
he turned to the taunting cocksure
multitude of forty-five
miscellaneous straight men preoccupied by musculature
and scores of conquest
tight men tight against gay
rights gay everything around them gay
hey/whatever happened to
dictatorship
anyway
next thing you know and your dog will be gay
and your wife and the cop on the corner gay gay
teachers in the classroom gay
victim of aids gay soldiers
in uniform gay fathers
of children gay
athletes on the U.S. Olympic teams
of whatever gay
members of the city council gay
lovers who love themselves gay
mothers gay
brothers-in-law gay
nuns gay priests gay
gay T.W.A. pilots gay
lumberjacks
gay rockstars gay
gay revolutionaries they
were saying, "Enough
enough!"
when he
in the gym
by himself
this Black homosexual this man
took on the question: *if not here then where if not now*—
And he spoke to them saying:
"Okay! Look at me!" And in front of them he stood
thinking
they should march into a stadium

and gathering there by the hundreds
tear out their eyes
that they might no longer see him or
me/this despicable growing minority
here
outside but gathered as strong as we stand.
They should tear out their eyes
so the world will look only
the way they believe to be
beautiful!
Because
we are everywhere
gay
and today you just can't be sure
anymore
who's who
or
what's what
now
can you?

But they did not move they
did not say anything and they broke
into the locker of this Black homosexual this
human being and they broke they smashed his glasses
that let him deal
real
among the gay and the grim
and he left that gym
by himself

In that same beginning winter
when the first rivers burst torrential
to attack to overcome
the limitations of all compromise

he slipped into the rising up
we who will irreversibly see
and name our own destiny
with our own
open eyes

Smash the Church

I am eating
I am eating ⅔s of a half pound of cashew nuts
dry roasted
filling the cavity full
with cashew nuts
because I still don't understand
why I wanted to win so much
I hit my nine-year-old
best friend
because she didn't feel like playing
ball
softball
on the day of the final play-offs
for the championship of Central Valley
New York
okay
I was nine years old
but so what
and I knew we couldn't win without her
and she Jodi
played third base I think
and didn't hit me back she
hit that ball
pretty damn good
and we won
nothing to take home
nothing to wear
nothing to eat

I am eating ⅔s of a half pound of cashew nuts
dry roasted
filling the cavity full
with cashew nuts
because I still don't get it
why I had to hit her
why we had to win
that game
I wish that I could burn my hand
I can't because I am

a coward
just like any intermittent psychopath
salivating hellbent towards whatever
she wants
she tells herself
I want that so I need
fresh raspberries in December
⅔s of a half pound of cashew nuts
I am eating them
because I want to
        I need to
eat them
up
devour the itch the tickle
the pinch the probing pierce elements of my
appetite
because I still don't understand it
because I still don't understand it
I am eating
I am eating ⅔s of a half pound of cashew nuts
        I can't figure out why
I thought another friend of mine was weird
or funny
see
because she offered me
some bread
not fancy
not nut
not spice
but bread
one loaf of plain bread
hot from a bakery we
passed by
why did I turn shy
against the basic thing
that bread
that we might choose as something
rare
something precious we could share
like soldiers?

Food will fortify your body:
Where's the war?

I am eating
I am eating ⅔s of a half pound of cashew nuts
not bread
I am writing this tonight although I could be eating
with a friend instead
because I still don't understand my
appetite
what's wrong with bread
what's nuts about these nuts
what's right about this poem in my head
        does monopoly capital fit
into it
I'm sorry that I hit
my best friend
And the basic story of the basic loaf of bread
will not end
here

Take: Eat,
This is My Body
I wish that I could burn my hand.
The body of Christ.
The bread of heaven.

Jodi
pushed away
the movie magazine that she'd been reading
and she said
straight and simple
as   daily bread,
"Okay.
Let's play."

The game is still a test of grace.

Raspberries in December
Thin wafer and thick wine
The blood shed
so that the hungry could recognize and savor
basic bread.

We wish that we could win

against the furies of original
unalterable sin.

The trouble with church
is
somebody has to let you in and
nobody knows how
to let you out.
However
cashew nuts do not
conclusively
attest to crime
and ceremonies of self-hatred
do not truly make you
beautiful.

Dear Jodi
from as long ago as bubble gum
I come
apology in hand

I know it's good
at last
I say it's possible
at least
to let the bad stuff go

Don't Estimate!

I need to know
exactly
how many stars separate Brooklyn from the Rockies
How many light years filled with what
passionate ash will float
into a visible position
blazing liberties of tenderness
to captivate the Denver sky

I do not detect the fragile
morning stars
that smile with my confusion
I cannot see the molten
or ethereal trace recollections
of this into-my-body experience
expanding circular canopies
of planets ruled by lust
as welcome
as suddenly regular
as daybreak

But I am found by fantasies
that even here
on the third floor walk-up of a city hideaway
may force me
down into indifferent urban
circumstances that include (I hope!)
a near by travel agent ready/
waiting
on my urgent lover's
trust

"Financial Planning"
(A poem commissioned by Forbes magazine)

Fifty cents more an hour would get me
  a house in the country
  hilarious friends calling
  an airedale that wakes up only for brunch
  a lover lusting insatiate
  liberation from my own daily routines
10,000 more a year would get me
  in debt for the house in the country
  part of the car that will slide up the driveway
  tennis lessons in the neighborhood
  installment plan travel out of that
  neighborhood entirely

an A-1 recommended kennel for my dog
50,000 beyond that would get me
a whole lotta trouble
I'm sure
for example
I would have to revise this poem
and I don't know
how

Poem for Mark

England, I thought, will look like Africa
or India with elephants and pale men
pushing things about
rifle and gloves
handlebar mustache and tea
pith helmets
riding crop
The Holy Bible
and a rolled up map of plunder
possibilities

But schoolboys with schoolbags
little enough for sweets
wore Wellingtons into the manicured
mud
and Cockney manners
("I say
we've been waiting 45 minutes
for this bus, we 'ave! It's
a regular disgrace,
it 'tis!"
"Yes, love: I'm sorry! But
step up/move along,
now! I'm doing the best I can!
You can
write a letter if you please!")
quite outclassed the Queen's

And time felt like a flag
right side up and flying
high while mousse-spike haircuts
denim jackets strolled around
and Afro-Caribbean/Afro-Celtic men
and women comfortable in full
length Rasta dreads
invited me to dinner or
presented me with poetry

And we
sat opposite but close
debating Nicaragua
or the civil liberties of countries
under siege
and you said
"Rubbish!" to the notion of a national
identity
and if I answered,
"In my country—"
You would interrupt me, saying,
"You're not serious!"
but then I thought I was
about "my country"
meaning where I'd come from
recently
and after only transatlantic static for a single
phone call
up against my loathing to disrupt and travel
to the silly land of Philip and Diana
never having hoped for anyone (a bebop-
antelope) like you
so quietly impertinent and teasing
it was 4 a.m. the first time
when we stopped the conversation
And long before my face lay nestling on the hotel
pillows/well
I knew
whoever the hell "my people"
are
I knew that one of them
is you

DeLiza Come to London Town
A Birthday Poem for Mark

DeLiza walk across the Waterloo
at night
She short but happy that she maybe have
one inch or two
on Bonaparte
who (anyway) look peculiar up against the backdrop
of Big Ben

She cogitate
on glory and the sword/she
smoke a cigarette among a hundred homeless
white men
them the Queen forget to decorate
with bed or blanket
softening the bottomline along the lamp-lit
dirty river

DeLiza race away from Waterloo
at night
She run she clutch she hotel key real tight:
DeLiza shaken from she speculation
on The Empire and The Crown:

> Them that will not kiss the family
> like as not to kill
> the strangers that they meet

DeLiza and the TV News

DeLiza watch one hostage then
she watch two hostage
then she think it must be
she descend

from something like that
only some may call it slavery and
a middle passage

DeLiza say you call it
what you want to
she think
the original hostage
holocaust kill some 22 million
African hostage
so they die

And somebody real popular
have high-jack that history
to this very day

Sometimes DeLiza

Sometimes DeLiza
she forget about location
and she wondering what to do
to make she Black self
just a little more
conspicuous

(She thinking
maybe she wear pink
or smoke a pipe)

But when she realize
she altogether in New Hampshire
not
The Planet

Then
DeLiza laugh out loud

War and Memory

Dedicated to Jane Creighton

I

Daddy at the stove or sink. Large
knife nearby or artfully
suspended by his clean hand handsome
even in its menace
slamming the silverware drawer
open and shut/the spoons
suddenly loud as the yelling
at my mother
no (she would say) no
Granville no
about: would he
be late/had she
hidden away the Chinese laundry shirts
again/did she think
it right that he (a man in his own house)
should serve himself a cup of tea a plate
of food/perhaps she thought that he
should cook the cabbage and the pot roast
for himself
as well?
It sure did seem she wanted him to lose
his job because she could not find
the keys
he could not find
and no (she would attempt to disagree)
no Granville no
but was he
trying to destroy her with his mouth
"My mouth?!" my Daddy hunkered down
incredulous and burly now
with anger, "What you mean, 'My mouth'?! You, woman!
  Who
you talk to in that way?
I am master of this castle!" Here
he'd gesture with a kitchen fork
around the sagging clutter
laugh and choke the rage tears
watering his eyes: "You no to speak to me

204

like that: You hear?
You damn Black woman!"
And my mother
backing up or hunching smaller
than frail bones should easily allow
began to munch on saltine
crackers
let the flat crumbs scatter on her full lips
and the oilcoth
on the table

"You answer me!" he'd scream, at last:
"I speak to you. You answer me!"
And she might struggle then
to swallow
or to mumble finally out loud:
"And who are you supposed to be? The Queen
of England? Or the King?"
And he
berserk with fury lifted
chair or frying pan
and I'd attack
in her defense: "No
Daddy! No!" rushing for his knees
and begging, "Please
don't, Daddy, please!"
He'd come down hard: My head
break into daylight pain
or rip me spinning crookedly across the floor.
I'd match him fast
for madness
lineage in wild display
age six
my pigtails long enough to hang me
from the ceiling
I would race about for weaponry
another chair a knife
a flowered glass
the radio
"You stop it, Daddy! Stop it!:
brandishing my arsenal
my mother
silently

beside the point.
He'd seize me or he'd duck the glass
"You devil child!
You damn Black devil child!"
"And what are you supposed to be?"
My mother might inquire
from the doorway:
"White? Are you supposed to be a white man
Granville?"
"Not white, but right!" And I would have to bite and kick
or race away
sometimes out the house and racing
still for blocks
my daddy chasing
after me

II
Daddy at the table reading
all about the Fiji Islanders or childhood
in Brazil
his favorite National Geographic research
into life beyond our
neighborhood
my mother looking into
the refrigerator
"Momma!" I cried, after staring at the front page
photo of The Daily News.
"What's this a picture of?"
It was Black and White,
But nothing else. No people
and no houses anywhere. My mother
came and took a look above my shoulder.
"It's about the Jews": she said.
"The Jews?"
"It's not! It's more about those Nazis!" Daddy
interjected.
"No, Granville, no!
It's about the Jews. In the war going on,"
my mother amplified, "the German soldiers
take away the Jewish families and they make
them march through snow until they die!"

"What kind of an ignorant
woman are you?" Daddy shouted out, "It's
not the snow. It's Nazi camps: the concentration
camps!"
"The camps?" I asked them, eagerly: "The Nazis?"
I was quite confused, "But in this picture,
Daddy, I can't see nobody."
"*Any*body," he corrected me: "You can't see
anybody!" "Yes, but what," I persevered, "what is this a
picture of?"
"That's the trail of blood left by the Jewish girls
and women on the snow because the Germans
make them march so long."
"Does the snow make feet bleed, Momma?
Where does the bleeding come from?"

My mother told me I should put away
the papers and not continue to upset myself
about these things I could not understand
and I remember
wondering if my family was a war
going on
and if
there would soon be blood
someplace in the house
and where
the blood of my family would come from

         III
The Spanish Civil War:
I think I read about that one.

         IV
Joan DeFreitas/2 doors up
she latched onto a soldier
fat cat bulging at the belt
and he didn't look like Hollywood
said he should
so I couldn't picture him defending
me or anyone

207

but then I couldn't picture war or North
Korea
at that time

                    V
There was tv
There were buses down to Washington, D.C.
You could go and meet your friends
from everywhere.
It was very exciting.
The tear gas burned like crazy.
The President kept lying to us.
Crowd counts at the rallies.
Body counts on the news.
Ketchup on the steps of universities.
Blood on the bandages around the head of the Vietnamese
women shot between the eyes.
Big guys.

Aerial spray missions.
Little people
Shot at close range
"Hell no! We won't go!"
"Hell no! We won't go!
Make love
Kill anything that moves.
Kent State.
American artillery unlimited at Jackson State
Who raised these devil children?
Who invented thse Americans with pony
tails and Afros and tee shirts and statistical
arguments against the mining of the harbors
of a country far away?

And I remember turning from the footage of the tat-tat-tat-
tat-tat-tat
helicopters
and I wondered how democracy would travel from the graves
at Kent State
to the hidden trenches
of Hanoi

208

VI

Plump during The War on Poverty
I remember making pretty good
money (6 bucks an hour)
as a city planner and my former
husband married my best
friend and I was never positive
about the next month's rent but
once I left my son sitting
on his lunchbox in the early rain
waiting for a day-care pickup and I went
to redesign low-income housing for the Lower
East Side of Manhattan and three hours after that
I got a phone call from my neighbors
that the pickup never came
that Christopher was waiting
on the sidewalk
in his yellow slicker
on his lunchbox
in the rain.

VII

I used to sometimes call the government
to tell them how my parents
ate real butter or stole sugar
from The Victory Rations
we received

I sometimes called the Operator
asking for Police
to beat my father up for beating me
so bad
but no one listened to
a tattletale
like me:

I think I felt relieved
because the government didn't send a rescue
face or voice to my imagination
and I hated
the police
but what else could you do?

Peace never meant a thing to me.

I wanted everyone to mold
the plastic bag for margarine
save stamps
plant carrots
and
(imitating Joe "Brown Bomber" Louis)
fight hard
fight fair
And from the freedom days
that blazed outside my mind
I fell in love
I fell in love with Black men White
men Black
women White women
and I
dared myself to say The Palestinians
and I
worried about unilateral words like Lesbian or Nationalist
and I
tried to speak Spanish when I travelled to Managua
and I
dreamed about The Fourteenth Amendment
and I
defied the hatred of the hateful everywhere
as best I could
I mean
I took long nightly walks to emulate the Chinese
    Revolutionaries
and I
always wore one sweater less than absolutely necessary to
    keep warm

and I wrote everything I knew how to write against apartheid
and I
thought I was a warrior growing up
and I
buried my father with all of the ceremony all of the music
    I could piece together
and I
lust for justice

210

and I
make that quest arthritic/pigeon-toed/however
and I
invent the mother of the courage I require not to quit